"The role of the arts in a life of faith is a concept worth exploring. Through an examination of thought and practice, *The Arts and the Christian Life* invites us into this conversation, presenting ideas that resonated with my experience. I came away with a renewed hope regarding the merits of artistic practice, not as an aside to faith but as an integral part of living out salvation."

—LISA LYSACK,
visual artist

"'The soul is the form of forms,' said Joyce in *Ulysses*. Earl Davey, in *The Arts and the Christian Life*, philosophically examines the role of art in the life of the individual and in the church and attempts to answer the question of how art can be understood to shape the Christian soul in such a manner that it manifests a way of *being* in Christ."

—SALLY ITO,
Canadian Mennonite University

"Few things are more perplexing to the congregation than the role of beauty in worship. Why does beauty matter? Does beauty lead us to God? Who decides whether something is beautiful and according to what criteria? In this illuminating book, Earl Davey guides us through major themes in the field of aesthetics, explaining at each stage of the argument how and why great music, painting, and poetry lead us into the beauty of holiness."

—DAVID WIDDICOMBE,
former rector, St. Margaret's Anglican Church

"Davey conducts his readers faithfully through philosophical nuances of aesthetics and the value of the arts raised throughout Western civilization's discourse. Most eloquent is Davey's evocation of mankind's need to strive for richer meaning and purpose, to 'revel in the magnificence of the creation, and in the joy . . . found in creating.'"

—**Karen Holland,**
teacher and visual artist

"Lyrical, passionate, and persuasive, Davey's argument for the embrace of the arts as a way to experience greater wholeness and joy in the Christian walk will be welcome for anyone seeking to reconcile serious faith with serious artistry. The fruit of a lifetime of devotion, musical engagement, philosophical reflection, and teaching, it ought to stimulate debate in classrooms, greenrooms, and vestries regarding the extent to which God reveals himself through great works of art."

—**Yuri Hooker,**
principal cello, Winnipeg Symphony Orchestra,
and associate pastor, Bethesda Church

The Arts and the Christian Life

THE ARTS AND THE CHRISTIAN LIFE

EARL DAVEY

WIPF & STOCK · Eugene, Oregon

THE ARTS AND THE CHRISTIAN LIFE

Copyright © 2022 Earl Davey. All rights reserved. Except for brief quotations in critical publications or reviews, no part of this book may be reproduced in any manner without prior written permission from the publisher. Write: Permissions, Wipf and Stock Publishers, 199 W. 8th Ave., Suite 3, Eugene, OR 97401.

Wipf & Stock
An Imprint of Wipf and Stock Publishers
199 W. 8th Ave., Suite 3
Eugene, OR 97401

www.wipfandstock.com

PAPERBACK ISBN: 978-1-6667-3331-0
HARDCOVER ISBN: 978-1-6667-2784-5
EBOOK ISBN: 978-1-6667-2785-2

MAY 2, 2022 8:36 AM

Scripture quotations are from the *New Revised Standard Version Bible*, copyright © 1989 National Council of Churches of Christ in the United States of America. Used by permission. All rights reserved worldwide.

This book is for Marion Dick Davey
and our children: Jordan Potter Davey,
Harrison James Davey, and Rachael Davey Loeppky.

Quantum potes, tantum aude.
Dare to do as much as you are able.

Contents

Acknowledgments | ix
Introduction | xi

1. THE SPIRITUAL SIGNIFICANCE OF ART AND BEAUTY | 1
2. BEAUTY | 13
3. EMOTION AND THE ARTS | 37
4. FORMALISM REVISITED AND REVISED | 59
5. METAPHOR AND MUSICAL EXPERIENCE | 82
6. MUSIC AND IMAGINATION | 109
7. ART, BEAUTY, AND THE CHRISTIAN LIFE | 124
8. EPILOGUE | 139

Bibliography | 143

Acknowledgments

This book would not have been completed without the support and encouragement of my dear wife, Marion Dick Davey.

I also wish to thank the staff of the Ralph Pickard Bell Library, Mount Allison University, for their kind assistance in the latter stages of my research and writing. In particular I am grateful for the assistance of Laura Landon, Head, Access Services and Interlibrary Loans; as well as Keagan Hawthorne, Susan Duke, and Rodney Howland.

Introduction

THE CHRISTIAN JOURNEY OF becoming more fully human, of experiencing a broader and deeper life of the mind and the spirit, involves striving to embrace all of one's being—one's spiritual, intellectual, and emotional life. A central assumption that underlies this collection of essays is that this journey toward fullness is abetted by engagement with significant works of art, for in exploring and contemplating these imaginative worlds of music, literature, poetry, art, and architecture (among others), we encounter and participate in the beautiful, which points beyond itself to the very goodness and beauty of God.

Foundational to the human enterprise is the search for meaning. Hence our engagements with works of art are typically laden with questions concerning where value is found and how meaning and import are understood and experienced. For persons of Christian faith, a parallel question arises concerning the significance such experience holds for the Christian life and the spiritual journey. The following essays pursue questions that address how it is we perceive value in our experience of the arts, how this experience leads to a greater measure of human fullness, and what significance engagement with the arts holds for the Christian life. The treatment one encounters here of music and the other arts is consequently both philosophical and theological, where the theological commentary is, for the most part, concerned with an applied theology, that is, with the spiritual life, with the mystery of faith and communion with God through engagement with the beautiful. I argue that human experience and the quality of our personhood is enriched in and through our imaginative life and that our spiritual lives are profoundly impacted by our aesthetic engagements. An underlying assumption is that great music, painting, and literature—indeed, all great art—is inherently religious: that is, they embody qualities

Introduction

that reflect the glory of God and are therefore valuable to the Christian life and one's spiritual experience.

As to its readership, this volume is addressed primarily to undergraduates and lay readers rather than to specialists who are either philosophers or theologians. The essays that are philosophically framed are written to be accessible to a broad audience; and, likewise, the theological reflections are directed not primarily to theologians but first of all to lovers of music and the arts who seek a better understanding of how meaning or import is constructed and ascribed to art works and how experience of these things may be reconciled with the spiritual life.

It must also be noted that this work focuses principally on music and musical experience because it is my discipline and life work. That said, it is hoped and intended that much, if not most, of what is ascribed to musical experience pertains across the arts—to literature, poetry, painting, sculpture, theater, dance, etc. Finally, I would add that these essays are located within what might be called the tradition of Western Christendom and do not address the music and art of other great cultures and religious traditions.

As to the structure of the book, the first chapter introduces the idea of the challenge encountered in the Christian life to become more than one now is, to strive toward a richer and fuller experience of what it is to be human, created in God's image, and to see this as part of one's spiritual journey toward Christ and the unique identity God has made possible for each of us. I then turn to several of the key concepts and interpretive lenses through which we perceive and interpret our experience of art and consider what impact art may have in the Christian life, beginning with a treatment of the concept of beauty (ch. 2) and the suggestion that engagement with music and the other arts, insofar as the arts constitute the beautiful and the good, offers a means by which we participate in a rich and fecund imaginative world that leads to a fuller and more complex human experience and opportunity for encounter with the Divine.

This is followed by an exploration of the idea that the principal value of art lies in its capacity to give expression to human feeling and emotion and explores ways in which music in particular is said to stand in relation to emotion (ch. 3). While I argue that music does not constitute a language, I explore a variety of theorists, including Suzanne Langer, who consider how music might be understood to have significance and import without having meaning as such. This treatment of emotion theory underscores the human inclination to make connections, transferences, and associations between

Introduction

one thing and another in order to construct meaning of our human experience. With respect to music and, indeed, other arts, we often see and hear insinuations and allusions to other domains of our experience, including our experience of God.

In the fourth chapter, we consider the idea of music and the other arts as modes of significant form and the notion that their value lies in the form of their presentation and not in anything they may be said to represent, evoke, or mean. This formalist view hearkens back to the second chapter on beauty theory, which very much rests on the formal pattern and qualities of the work as a basis for the work's designation as the beautiful. This exploration is paired with a consideration of what is involved in making sense of and interpreting the artistic worth of a work: that is to say, it explores the place of the cognitive in aesthetic activity and how reason is seen to interface with the aesthetic, including the question of what it is to know or appreciate something intuitively.

The fifth chapter returns to the idea that in our engagement with the arts, the mind and imagination move very quickly to interrelate one thing with another, to make connections and points of transfer. This chapter, like the chapter addressing emotion theory, privileges music among the arts in its treatment of the ways in which we construct meaning of metaphor and the role of metaphor in musical perception.

The sixth chapter addresses the role of the imagination in the aesthetic process, a process in which the percipient or performer engages with the musical work in order to realize the work, that is, to construct a sound image that accounts for both the straightforward facts of the score along with its contingent features. This exploration focuses on the interpretive and analytical process involved in understanding a work and what is there to be heard. It explores the significance of this imaginative experience in leading one to artful practice and the pleasure taken in the artful and the beautiful. I suggest that this movement toward the work in its fullness is a movement toward that which is beautiful and good, and therefore also toward the holy.

The penultimate chapter considers the idea of art and artistry as gift and sacrifice and treats the question of how we are able to offer our talents and the products of our imagination to God and to the church as a gift and also as a sacrifice of our labor. This essay returns to the theme introduced in the first chapter—the contribution of the aesthetic and the artistic to the Christian life and to the process of personal and spiritual transformation. The book concludes with a brief epilogue.

Introduction

Each of the chapters, apart from the first and the epilogue, concludes with a section entitled "Notes for the Church," which offers a theological reflection exploring the significance of the preceding material to the Christian life.

In summary, this book is written to enable those who love and engage with the arts, most particularly with music, to understand more fully the value of such experience, and to assist in effecting a more intentional integration of this experience in the spiritual journey.

1

The Spiritual Significance of Art and Beauty

INTRODUCTION: THE ARTS AND THEIR VALUE

The human species, created in the image of God as told in the ancient wisdom of the Genesis text, is marked in many and diverse ways as God's own: by its purposiveness toward knowing and toward freedom; its capacity for reason, imagination, hope, love, loyalty, self-reflection, and self-sacrifice; and, above all, its desire to encounter and know God. These defining qualities of humanness are reflected in our literature, music, poetry, painting, sculpture, dance, and rituals—the practices and structures by which we reflect upon and cultivate our capacity for hope, love, and charity. These are the tools we use to explore the essential features of our humanness and give expression to our striving to become more than we now are. Through these forms and mechanisms, we give voice to our prayer and praise, our love and longing for God, and both the good and destructive things of this world.

These products of mind and the human imagination contribute to what we speak of as culture, to the multiple cultures across time and space that are the footprints of our common humanity. They mark our humanness. These forms and symbols record our joys, sorrows, and triumphs; they stand as evidence of our need of redemption and transformation. But they also constitute magnificent products of the human imagination that have the markings of beauty, that point toward the Divine, and reflect the glory of God. It is my working assumption that engagement with such works is a means of cultivating a greater measure of fullness of our human experience, a fullness that God desires and makes possible for us. This search for fulfilment, I argue, is part of the process of our spiritual journey as Christians, part of coming to know and experience God through engagement with art and the beautiful—a process that involves the exercise of our minds and the engagement of our hearts in faith. To this end, this volume addresses some of the ways in which we attempt to make sense of the arts and our experience of these various forms, and we consider the question of their significance in the Christian life.

I have spoken already of music, literature, poetry, painting, sculpture, and dance collectively as representing part of what is yet a more extensive set of artistic forms that are commonly denoted as the arts or fine arts. Let us begin by recognizing that the word *art* is now utilized in such a manner that it is impossible to establish boundaries that can be defensibly applied to the term. Moreover, when we consider the range of artistic forms, each with its particular materials, compositional techniques, and conventions, the difficulty of determining what, if anything, unites them becomes all the more evident. Yet these multiple and disparate art forms have long been viewed as a set, possessing some unifying principle or philosophical intent. Part of the work of philosophical speculation in the field of aesthetics focuses on the problems of how art is to be defined, why it is important, where its value lies, and what contribution it makes to human experience. In response to such questions, the philosophical community has developed various theories of art, several of which are examined in this work, including art as beauty, art as expression of human feeling and emotion, and art as significant form. In this context, we are also interested in what may be seen as a parallel question, a theological question that centers on the significance of the arts in the Christian life and spiritual experience. To this purpose, we turn to the American Jesuit theologian Alejandro Garcia-Rivera who poses a somewhat different question. Garcia-Rivera asks, "What moves the human heart?" This reframing of the philosophical orientation of questions pertaining to art and its value is critical, because it recognizes the spiritual nature of humankind and invites a method of inquiry into the value of art and aesthetic experience that is both philosophical and theological: where the two postures at various points intersect and together inform how we might better understand the place of the arts, artistic and aesthetic activity, in our society and, more particularly, in Christian experience and the life of the church. These, then, constitute the broad purposes of this work.

The Spiritual Significance of Art and Beauty

In this introductory chapter, I begin with a brief exploration of the idea of what it is to become more than we now are. What does this spiritual journey of the Christian entail, and what place does engagement with the arts have in this transformative process?

BEAUTY: A PATHWAY TO GOD

In pursuit of personal and spiritual development, some choose a path that focuses principally on the reading of the biblical and spiritual texts, in the context of a life of prayer and contemplation. But the fact is that the life of the true ascetic and contemplative is a calling of the few. For most of us, the spiritual journey of which we speak includes these foundational elements of prayer and contemplation but draws upon a much broader range of elements. Inasmuch as we are created in God's image with all the capacities, proclivities, and possibilities accorded to self-conscious and rational beings, we rightly assume that the exploration of imaginative and artistic worlds is part of the good and abundant life that God has made possible and intends for his people. The riches and glory of language, literature, and poetry, of mathematics, painting, sculpture, music, and dance—all of this is part of the bounty and mercy of God—gifts of God for his creation and his people. All of this is part of the spiritual life and journey in which we find ourselves drawn closer to God.

The exploration and cultivation of the mind as part of the stewardship of the intellectual resources that are ours have long been important to the life of the Christian church, as evidenced by the work of the great religious colleges and universities that emerged under the church's auspices. In the West, one thinks of the University of Bologna, the oldest university in Europe, established in 1088. While initially dedicated to training in canon and civil law, by the end of the fourteenth century, the university had added to its curriculum the study of medicine, philosophy, arithmetic, astronomy, logic, rhetoric, and grammar. Theology was added to the curriculum only in the mid-fourteenth century. The founding of the University of Paris followed in the second half of the twelfth century. The earliest of the Oxford Colleges—University, Balliol, and Merton Colleges—emerged in the following century. In 1347, Pope Clement VI established a university in Prague, which was followed by the University of Heidelberg, the oldest university in Germany, in 1386. Over succeeding centuries, these institutions, along with many others scattered throughout Europe and the world, provided an enormous resource for the Christian church. Indeed, the church was the principal source of employment for university graduates, and the structure of the arts faculties was designed to meet their needs.

It is notable, however, that pursuit of the beautiful in terms of the study and creation of artifacts or artistic products was not principally the province of the universities, but of the guilds of the various arts and crafts, including masonry, gold and silver work, carpentry, weaving, glass work, and scores of other specialties. And of course, much of the finest of this work was commissioned by the churches and cathedrals throughout Europe. All of this is simply to note that stewardship of the mind and human imagination, and the practice of artistry and production of the beautiful, has long been part of the discipline of the Christian community.

Traditionally, the Christian community has assumed that it gives glory to God through the exercising of its talents and artistic capacities. Since the early Middle Ages and earlier yet, it built libraries containing the knowledge and research of all the known world; it cultivated the artistic abilities needed to produce magnificent books beautifully illustrated and decorated; it erected churches, cathedrals, and monasteries, all of which evidenced the artistic capacities and aesthetic sensibilities of the community. This labor of the heart and mind, labor that extended far beyond the reach of the ordinary and that which was functionally necessary, was done to the greater glory of God. The flourish that marked such labor was not taken as mere vanity but as a joyous expression of the bounty of the human spirit dedicated to God, the giver of all good gifts. This dedication to excellence of mind and refined craft was understood as a proper part of the spiritual life of the community, along with the community's prayers and spiritual readings. The liturgy of the church was itself a thing of beauty. The Gregorian chant of the chapels and monastic choirs resounded in beautifully constructed spaces, with alters and naves resplendent with carved and painted figures, and scenes depicting the saints of the church and the biblical narrative. Whether in a simple country chapel or a magnificent cathedral, the life of faith was given expression in the worship of the church—a worship that exhibited the artistry of the church and the community as part of its spiritual service and witness to the glory of God. The work and life of the church has been formed and colored by poetry, literature, music, painting, architecture, and the combination of these various arts in the ritual of the church throughout its history and across cultures.

The Spiritual Significance of Art and Beauty

As we shall see in our subsequent examination of beauty theory, and particularly in the writings of Thomas Aquinas, the Christian community has long held the view that participation in the beautiful constitutes action that is good. While most of the philosophical community has long abandoned the language of the beautiful and the concept of beauty as a quality of God and an essential feature of being, a deep commitment to the idea of the beautiful continues to be evidenced in the contemporary theological aesthetics of many, including Hans Urs von Balthasar, *Seeing the Form* (1982); James Alfred Martin Jr., *Beauty and Holiness: The Dialogue between Aesthetics and Religion* (1990); Patrick Sherry, *Spirit and Beauty: An Introduction to Theological Aesthetics* (1992); John Navone, *Towards a Theology of Beauty* (1996); Richard Viladesau, *Theological Aesthetics: God in Imagination, Beauty and Art* (1999); Alejandro Garcia-Rivera, *The Community of the Beautiful: A Theological Aesthetics* (1999), and Edward Farley, *Faith and Beauty: A Theological Aesthetic* (2001). Among such voices is that of Pope Benedict XVI. In 2008, at a retreat for the priests of the Diocese of Bolzano-Bressanone held at the Cathedral of S. Maria Assunta, Benedict spoke to the matter of the beautiful and the Christian life: "If we contemplate the beauties created by faith, they are simply . . . the living proof of faith." He proceeds to say: "If I look at this beautiful cathedral—it is a living proclamation! It speaks to us itself, and on the basis of the cathedral's beauty, we succeed in visibly proclaiming God, Christ and all his mysteries: here they have acquired a form and look at us." He then makes an altogether remarkable statement: "All the great works of art, cathedrals—the Gothic cathedrals and the splendid Baroque churches—they are all a luminous sign of God and therefore truly a manifestation, an epiphany of God." Benedict elaborates on this theme when he speaks of the music of the church: "We have just heard the organ in its full splendour. I think the great music born in the church makes the truth of our faith audible and perceivable: from Gregorian chant . . . to Palestrina . . . to Bach and hence to Mozart and Bruckner . . . we suddenly understand it is true! Wherever such things are born, the Truth is there."[1]

The assertion that all great works are a luminous sign of God and therefore truly a manifestation, an epiphany, of God is a striking statement. Benedict includes in this assertion all great works, sacred and secular. Moreover, he affirms the arts as a milieu in which "heart and reason encounter one another, beauty and truth converge." He concludes by encouraging the

1. Benedict XVI, "Meeting of Holy Father."

The Arts and the Christian Life

community of faith "to seek to ensure that the two categories, the aesthetic and the noetic (intellectual), are united and that in this great breadth the entirety and depth of our faith may be made manifest."[2] It is Benedict's view that an integration of the aesthetic, the creative, and artistic with a theology that privileges words and reason will lead to a greater depth in our faith and faith experience. Moreover, his embrace of all great art implies a rejection of the notion that only religious art holds value for the community of the faithful.

While Benedict affirms the theological and spiritual significance of great art, one remembers that the church has evidenced considerable ambiguity and, at times, outright hostility to the arts over the centuries. Most famously we recall Augustine's assertion that a love of literature distracted him from God: "What is more pitiable than a wretch without pity for himself who weeps over the death of Dido dying for love of Aeneas, but not weeping over himself dying for his lack of love for you, my God."[3] One finds similar expressions of concern regarding the seductiveness of the arts in the medieval writers. Eco, in his discussion of "the medieval aesthetic sensibility," refers to a Cistercian statute that "prohibited the use in churches of silk, gold, silver, paintings, stained glass, and carpets."[4] Importantly, Eco takes pains to make the point that these constraints were not evidence of a distain of beauty but a recognition of the seductive force of these things that elicit what Hugh of Fouilloi referred to as "a wondrous but perverse delight."[5] In the words of St. Bernard of Clairvaux, these things, "fair to see or soothing to hear, sweet to smell, delightful to taste, or pleasant to touch,"[6] these delights of the flesh, which, in his mind, included the iconography and elaborate architecture of the church, were beauties of the world that needed to be rejected for Christ's sake, for the sake of the humility, poverty, and simplicity appropriate to the Christian life. This view has continued to hold a place over the centuries in the minds of many across the entire structure of the church, Catholic and Protestant.

Despite the church's conflicted history concerning the arts and their place in the Christian life, we who have experienced joy, contentment, and wonder through engagement with the beautiful find no comfort in the suggestion that this engagement is in any sense inconsequential or merely

---

2. Benedict XVI, "Meeting of Holy Father."
3. Augustine, *Confessions*, 15.
4. Eco, *Aesthetics of Thomas Aquinas*, 7.
5. Hugh of Fouilloi, as cited in Eco, *Aesthetics of Thomas Aquinas*, 7.
6. Eco, *Aesthetics of Thomas Aquinas*, 7.

carnal. This is no "perverse delight" in the things of the flesh. In fact, our experience and common sense suggest otherwise. We know that the cultivation and experience of joy, contentment, and wonder are central to what we often call "the good life." Contemplation of the beautiful and the play of the mind in response to the imaginatively compelling are not incidental processes but events essential to life, events that take human experience beyond the routine and the ordinary. The arts do not merely offer a distraction from the real and important concerns of life; they are vital to the development of the imagination and the senses, vital to the process of becoming more fully human. To participate in the beautiful is to inhabit a garden of the mind and spirit in which it is possible to witness the goodness, beauty, and glory of the Lord. So, we stand in accord with Pope Benedict, recognizing and rightly affirming that the beautiful points us to God, that the wonder and joy we experience in the arts is itself a blessed thing, and that in the presence of the beautiful we at times find ourselves in the very presence of the Spirit of God.

As such, we hold that aesthetic activity bears, or has the potential to bear, a significant spiritual value, for it is a pathway, or, better yet, it contributes to a milieu in which those who have eyes to see and ears to hear may engage with the Divine. Indeed, the longing and desire we experience for the beautiful mirrors our longing for God. To experience the fullness our humanity promises necessitates an intimate connection with God. What is asserted here is that artistic and aesthetic activity is one of the pathways that God has provided for the church to experience his presence and a measure of his glory.

BECOMING MORE

Søren Kierkegaard once said that he took it to be an ethical imperative "that every man is born in such a condition that he can become one."[7] He refers to the potential of all humankind to become more than what it is and implies that much of our personal existence is marked by a mental and spiritual poverty. Aquinas also spoke of our potential to become fully human and of the *inclination* of all humanity to seek fulfilment (though, for Aquinas, to become fully human was to transcend the life of the flesh through the life of the spirit and become more like God). Of a certainty, one of the marks of humanity is the inclination to fulfilment, the propensity to become more

---

7. Kierkegaard, as quoted in Hannay, *Kierkegaard*, 314.

fully human. Admittedly, we often miss the mark as we struggle toward a fuller human experience, largely as a consequence of mistaking where true value lies. It is perhaps the common inclination to substitute the temporal for the eternal that causes Aquinas to argue for human fulfilment largely, if not exclusively, in spiritual terms. For it seems we are inclined most frequently to perceive the "good life" in terms of the temporal rather than the eternal, in terms of material and personal comforts and the approbation of others.

The Scriptures and the writings of the divines point in a different direction—the way of purity of heart and of a longing for a fuller knowledge and experience of God. But it is important to note that this kind of "becoming" embraces all domains of our lives—the intellectual, emotional, ethical, and spiritual facets of our being. It involves a transformation of mind and spirit, thought, feeling, and action that needs to be understood both in terms of salvation and the ongoing transformation of the person through the work of the Spirit of God. So, Saint Paul exhorts the church at Philippi to "work out your own salvation with fear and trembling; for it is God who is at work in you, enabling you both to will and to work for his good pleasure" (Phil 2:12–13), making it clear that this transformation is an ongoing process involving human agency and responsibility in partnership with the work of the Holy Spirit.

As we pursue this transformation from the ordinary and commonplace in this world of flesh, of dust and ashes, we need to consider how it is that the Spirit of God speaks to us. The ancient Hebraic text says, "The mountains and the hills before you shall burst into song, and all the trees of the field shall clap their hands" (Isa 55:12). The very mountains and hills praise the God of creation, and we are witness to this. This created world, this earthly paradise, offers poignant evidence of the love and presence of God. This love, embodied and revealed in God's creation, is found in form and color, image and concept, cause and relation, the purity of disinterested reason, in feeling, emotion, and human relationships. These graces of God were not confined to Eden. As we stand, conscious and self-aware in the midst of the glory of God's great work, we are in fact very often aware, intensely aware, of the profound disjunction between that which is possible and that which is. Between what I now am and that which I wish to become. Between the reality of my existence and the potential of my being as one of God's creations. The process of striving to become is a specifically human enterprise, the object of which is the joy of finding one's identity in Christ, in knowing God and experiencing the bounty of his grace. These graces,

The Spiritual Significance of Art and Beauty

I argue, include God's gifts to us of the beautiful, constructs not only of nature but of human hands and the human imagination.

That which is specifically human, including artistic and aesthetic activity, encompasses the theological, the ethical, and the spiritual; it involves relations between persons, between societies, between humankind and God. This process of becoming fully human, as I have put it, is not a private concern, not a purely individualistic process but one that must be pursued in a social and cultural context. It involves an existence in which the individual is responsible before God and members of his or her community for actions, attitudes, and relationships that are always more than personal and private, and for the development and utilization of one's potentialities for the benefit of others as well as oneself. This pursuit of fullness and consideration of the contribution of the arts to our becoming is best accomplished in the life and heart of the church, because the process is always and essentially spiritual in nature.

As a Christian community, we need to embrace the value of music and the other arts—that is, all artistic and aesthetic experience that is good and worthy. We need to cultivate an imaginative life and provide opportunity for the experience of the imaginative products of others whose life experience and ability is broader and greater than our own. Northrop Frye once said, it is the imagination that permits the transformation of the world as it is to the world as we wish it to be.[8] It is this process of transformation that lies at the heart of every culture—its literature, music, dance, architecture, painting, sculpture, and all other activity by which humankind transforms its physical, social, intellectual, and spiritual environment. The transformation of the self, of one's society, is the concern of all people. As such, artistic and aesthetic experience ought not be viewed as a peripheral concern in the Christian community. It is not, nor should it ever become, the domain of an elite or privileged group. The joy, wonder, and contentment that participation in these rich and complex imaginative worlds provides constitute a mode of human goodness that cannot be denied. For the Christian, this process of becoming more fully human, including the enrichment of the mind and imagination, is part of a human journey, a spiritual journey toward our true identity.

Pierre Teilhard de Chardin, in *The Divine Milieu*, makes the point that many are inclined to view the Christian life as constituted of that which is sacred over against that which is secular or profane. The Christian who

---

8. Frye, *Educated Imagination*, 4.

subscribes to such a dualism must ask whether that which is essentially profane or secular can have intrinsic value. Can it have spiritual value? This way of perceiving the Christian life not only affects the question of the significance of the arts and aesthetic engagement but all other activities viewed as secular or worldly. As a result of seeing the world this way, many devout Christians struggle with the significance of their daily occupation and often find it difficult to invest fully in their work, because that work, perceived as secular, is therefore of little eternal consequence. The same would apply to any work or engagement in that which is seen as worldly, or temporal. Teilhard recommends that the Christian shun this bifurcated view of the Christian life, arguing that, in Christ, life is a seamless whole, where Christ is in all.

Teilhard argues that Christ "the incarnate God did not come to diminish in us the glorious responsibility and splendid ambition that is ours: *of fashioning our own self.*"[9] This I take to have enormous import for the way in which the Christian understands his or her purpose and identity in this world as one created in God's image with talents, abilities, interests, and proclivities that mark one as an individual. As Christians, we affirm the joy and peace of God found in acts of spiritual devotion such as prayer and meditation on the Scriptures, and we affirm these things as essential in the process of coming to know God and coming to a place of greater fullness in our human experience. At the same time, we submit that God's intent with respect to humanity encompasses the entirety of our nature. Our imaginative and creative capacities are defining features of our humanity, which cannot be denied and should not be denigrated. The fundamental error of materialism and hedonism lies not in appreciation of the beautiful but in the failure to see Christ as the source of beauty and all other perfections.

Our fullness, our happiness and joy, are God's great pleasure. The sanctification of all we have is our sacrifice of praise and thanks to God for his great mercy and love. There is no logical or necessary division of life into sacred and secular when Christ is in all. There need be no exclusion of pursuit of the beautiful as a consequence of an exhortation to holiness when all that is done is done unto God in recognition of the lordship of Christ.

---

9. Teilhard de Chardin, *Divine Milieu*, 70; emphasis in original.

The Spiritual Significance of Art and Beauty

NOTES FOR THE CHURCH

Though self-evident, it needs to be said that aesthetic and artistic engagement represent only part, perhaps a very small part, of the process of spiritual becoming. No claim is made for art as a primary basis for spiritual transformation. As noted in our earlier reference to St. Paul's Letter to the Philippians, we are not conformed to the image of Christ through our own efforts, artistic or otherwise: "For it is God who is at work in you, enabling you both to will and to work for his good pleasure"(Phil 2:13). Yet, our striving is essential; in fact, it is a necessary condition of this becoming, as suggested by the New Testament images of running the race (Heb 12:1), fighting the good fight (2 Tim 4:7), and working out one's own salvation (Phil 2:12). This striving to become involves all of what we are and can be. It is not constituted of a set of activities limited to spiritual exercises. Such exercises have value only as a means to an end. For the Christian, the daily challenge to encounter Christ in all we do is no mere exercise. It is the very purpose of life. I speak here of becoming as a process of seeking fulfilment in the knowledge and experience of God and in the realization of the fullness of our humanity, which is God's gift to us, our very nature.

We are not, then, transformed by the beautiful, by art and artistry, in the biblical sense of being conformed to Christ; but we find in the beautiful the good. We discover in artful process activity that is affirming and pleasing to God as well as ourselves. As Christians, we seek to encounter God in doing the good, and these good things we understand as including acts of devotion such as prayer, fasting, meditation on the Scriptures, acts of public and collective worship. These good things also include engagement with the beautiful, whether the beauty of creation or the beauty of the human imagination. These good things include the praise we offer to God in consequence of the wonder and joy we find as we participate in the beautiful. As Teilhard has said (in connection with the subject of the building of the kingdom of God), "By virtue of the Creation and, still more, of the Incarnation, *nothing* here below is *profane* for those who know how to see."[10]

Kierkegaard, in his discussion of this process of becoming more fully human, places the ethical over the aesthetic in order of significance; moreover, he is inclined to view the latter as hedonistic. On this point, he is well aligned with many in the church who have taken this position. Without question, the Christian community, broadly speaking, has long experienced

---

10. Teilhard de Chardin, *Divine Milieu*, 66; emphasis in original.

a profound tension with respect to the arts. Is it not all vanity and ashes? I have argued that human fullness and this becoming that encompasses all of human nature and human potentialities is part of God's intent and design for humanity and for *his* church, and there is no need to recapitulate that argument here. But it is worth reiterating Chardin's assertion for our careful consideration: "The incarnate God did not come to diminish in us the glorious responsibility and splendid ambition that is ours: *of fashioning our own self*."[11] With respect to the arts and engagement with the beautiful, we do well to consider Pope Benedict's argument that an integration of the aesthetic, the creative and artistic, with a theology that privileges words and reason will lead to a greater depth in our faith and faith experience. The richness of our aesthetic and artistic lives does not stand in opposition to our spiritual existence. Rather, the mercies of God, the bounty of God's great blessing for us, include the beauty of the earth and the beauties of the mind.

> Praise the Lord!
> Praise God in his sanctuary;
> praise him in his mighty firmament!
> Praise him for his mighty deeds;
> praise him according to his surpassing greatness.
>
> Praise him with trumpet sound;
> praise him with lute and harp!
> Praise him with tambourine and dance;
> praise him with strings and pipe!
> Praise him with the clanging cymbals;
> praise him with loud clashing cymbals!
> Let everything that has breath praise the Lord!
> Praise the Lord! (Ps 150)

---

11. Teilhard de Chardin, *Divine Milieu*, 70; emphasis in original.

2

BEAUTY

INTRODUCTION

FROM THE TIME OF the ancient Greeks until the mid-eighteenth century, the concept of beauty has been foundational to philosophical speculation concerning the nature and value of music and all the creative arts. The beautiful was understood to constitute a whole, the parts of which were harmoniously interrelated, and characterized by the properties of unity and variety in unity, as well as the qualities of coherence, balance and symmetry. Several centuries after Plato and Aristotle, Plotinus offered a Platonic view of beauty as ideal-form: "Where the Ideal-Form has entered, it has grouped and coordinated what from a diversity of parts was to become a unity: it has rallied confusion into co-operation: it has made the sum one harmonious coherence: for the Idea is a unity and what it molds must come to unity as far as multiplicity may."[1]

In the thirteenth century, Thomas Aquinas formulated his understanding of the beautiful, adopting the formalistic framework of the Greeks. In the *Summa Theologiae*, we find beauty understood to involve three formal properties: integrity, proportion, and clarity. "First, integrity or perfection, for things that are lacking in something are for this reason ugly; also due proportion or consonance; and again, clarity, for we call things beautiful when they are brightly colored."[2] Like the Greeks, Aquinas understood beauty as involving an excellence of form. It was the perfection of form

---

1. Plotinus, *Enneads*, 47.
2. Aquinas, as translated by Eco, *Aesthetics of Thomas Aquinas*, 65.

that delighted the mind and the senses, and the excellence of an object was determined according to the criteria of integrity, proportion, and clarity.

Beginning in the mid-eighteenth century with the work of Alexander Baumgarten, the concept of beauty as an objective reality was both challenged and superseded by the idea of aesthetic perception, which involved a shift in focus from the status of the object as the locus of interest to the reception and experience of the work by its percipients. The work of Hume, Kant, and others had reconceived the long-standing view of beauty as an objective reality inherent in the work and substituted for it an understanding of beauty as a subjective quality dependent upon the perspective of the percipient. Notwithstanding the caveat that some judgments with respect to the beautiful and what qualified as beautiful ought to be understood as more valuable or reliable than others, the fact remained that beauty was essentially understood as a quality ascribed to works by their percipients. Accordingly, over time, beauty was no longer accepted as a foundational property and a basis for the ascribing of value to artworks. The alternative adopted by the philosophical community was to speak of the "aesthetic value" of artworks rather than of beauty. Though the language of subjectivist beauty persisted in the writings of Shaftesbury, Burke, Schiller, Schelling, Hegel, Schopenhauer, Hume, Kant, and many others, by the outset of the twentieth century, the concept of beauty advanced by the Greeks and the Scholastics had been thoroughly dismissed as inadequate in the face of questions such as whether there are in fact necessary and sufficient conditions that mark the existence of the beautiful, and whether the value of artworks could in fact be adequately accounted for by the concept of beauty. What of the ugly, the obscene, or the sublime? Are artworks characterized as such also understood as valuable, and, if so, can beauty be understood to be a sufficiently comprehensive construct to address the world of art?

What follows is a brief survey of the historical concept of beauty, with particular attention to the thought of Thomas Aquinas. Central to this discussion is an examination of the nature and value of the beautiful as the good and that which elicits pleasure and leads to happiness. Moreover, we explore what it may mean to participate in the "First Cause" through engagement with the beautiful, and the implications of this engagement on the formation of human identity and being. At the conclusion of the chapter, we return to a Thomistic view of the beautiful in the contemporary theological aesthetics of Balthasar, Viladesau, Navone, and Garcia-Rivera, which provide accounts of beauty as a quality of God and a foundational aspect of being.

BEAUTY AND THE GOOD

In the metaphysics of Plato, the relation between the good and the beautiful, or the good and the fine, is ambiguous. In the *Republic*, Plato asserts the appropriateness of assessing the beautiful by the standard of the good.[3] Again, in the *Symposium*, he substitutes the word *good* for *beautiful* when responding to the question, "What will this person have, if good things become his own?"[4] The answer given is that the possession of the good, and by implication the possession of the beautiful, results in happiness, for "happy people are happy through possessing good things."[5] In a similar vein, Aristotle, in *The Art of Rhetoric*, speaks of the relation of the beautiful to the good, where he says: "Both agreeable and beautiful things must be good; for the former produce pleasure, while among beautiful things some are pleasant and others are desirable in themselves."[6] While both argue that the beautiful must be good, that is not to say they are in fact identical. Rachel Barney serves as a useful guide to this puzzle, pointing us to a section of Plato's *Philebus* and the discussion of that which constitutes the happy.

> But now we notice that the force of the good has taken refuge in an alliance with the nature of the beautiful. For measure and proportion manifest themselves in all areas as beauty and virtue.
> —Undeniably.
> But we did say that truth is also included along with them in our mixture?
> —Indeed.
> Well, then, if we cannot capture the good in *one* form, we will have to take hold of it in a conjunction of the three: beauty, proportion, and truth. Let us affirm that these should by right be treated as a unity and be held responsible for what is in the mixture, for its goodness is what makes the mixture itself a good one.[7]

---

3. Plato, *Republic*, 148.
4. Plato, *Symposium*, 42.
5. Plato, *Symposium*, 43.
6. Aristotle, *Rhetoric*, 61.
7. Plato, as quoted in Barney, "Notes on Plato," 364.

Barney makes the point that while the language of the good "taking refuge" with the beautiful "suggests that the fine is something less than the good—yet it comes close enough to serve as a kind of proxy."[8] This partial conflation of the good and beautiful in the writings of Plato is a precursor and a foundation for the position of the Scholastics of the thirteenth century, including Aquinas, who viewed beauty as a mode of goodness.

It is also important to note that Plato viewed the beautiful as a quality or character of the object and not dependent for its existence upon the perceiving of it. This concept of the beautiful as an objective property of the object persisted in the West until the eighteenth century.[9]

During the Middle Ages, some of the most significant writing concerning the nature of beauty is found in the *Summa Theologiae* of Thomas Aquinas. Although influenced by the Greeks, Aquinas did not read Greek and had to access Greek texts through Latin translations and then only translations of fragments of text. His thought was also influenced by the Bible, the writings of Pythagoras, and the Neoplatonism of Proclus, Porphyry, and, most particularly, Dionysius the Areopagite.[10] Concerning the relation of the beautiful to the good, Aquinas, in response to Dionysius, argues that "Beauty and goodness in a thing are identical fundamentally; for they are based upon the same thing, namely, the form; and consequently goodness is praised as beauty."[11] With respect to the good and the nature of the good, Aquinas says, "*Per prius enim praedicatur de honesto; et secundario de delectabili; tertio de utili*," which translates as, "Hence it is predicated chiefly of the virtuous; then of the pleasant; and lastly of the useful."[12] Here, *honesto* may also be translated as "worthy," and *delectabili* as "delightful." Notice that something's utility is only a ground for ascribing a lesser value. The principal value of an object—a vase, for example—is not found in its utility, though such utility may not be irrelevant; more importantly, an object is beautiful as a consequence of its way of being, that is, because of its form.

Gerald Phelan, in "The Concept of Beauty in St. Thomas Aquinas," makes the point that Aquinas offers two definitions of beauty. One focuses on why things are called beautiful—"Beauty is said to be that which

---

8. Barney, "Notes on Plato," 364.

9. For an exposition of beauty as an objective quality and beauty theory in Plato, see Mothersill, *Beauty Restored*.

10. Eco, *Aesthetics of Thomas Aquinas*, 23.

11. Aquinas, *Summa Theologiae* 1, Q5, A4, ad. 1.

12. Aquinas, *Summa Theologiae* 1, Q5, A6, ad. 3.

pleases when seen"—and, secondly, on the formal, constituent properties of beauty: 1) completeness or perfection, 2) due proportion or harmony, 3) splendor. Phelan argues that *integritas* and *perfectio* refer to existence and being; *proportio* and *consonantia* to order, finality, and goodness; and *claritas* to knowledge, intelligibility, formality, and truth.[13] Accordingly, the three constituents of beauty are being, truth, and goodness.[14] In Phelan's reading, Aquinas is principally interested in beauty in a metaphysical sense; hence his interest focuses on beauty as form and on its connection with the good.

While Aquinas argues that beauty and goodness in a thing are fundamentally identical, he does offer a point of separation between the two which is of consequence to those interested in a theological aesthetic. Beauty, he argues, is a formal cause because it is cognitive and therefore not appetitive. The good, however, has the nature of a final cause, because the good is an object of desire and causes movement toward itself. The significance of this distinction between the beautiful and the good—the one as a cognitive force and a formal cause, the other as an appetitive force and a final cause—is underscored by Sevier in *Aquinas on Beauty*. For the purpose of clarifying the link between beauty and ethics, Sevier reminds the reader that, for Aquinas, beauty is tied to the good but also that the good is tied to appetite and desire. As agents created in God's image, we are called to desire the good. And so, in the mind of Aquinas, beauty is fundamentally linked with ethics. That is, beauty is linked with virtue; for, as Sevier puts it, "What we desire, therefore, shows what we take to be good."[15] So, as the virtues—prudence, justice, temperance and fortitude—"perfect the appetite, so our desires reflect the degree to which the soul has been conformed to right reason through the exercise of, and habituation in, the virtues."

Participation in the Beautiful: Participation in the First Cause

For many contemporary readers, the idea of the good as also beautiful is strange, for our concept of beauty is often limited to that which is pretty or attractive. Clearly, the concept to which Aquinas refers has little to do with beauty as mere ornament. In fact, it is not limited to the materiality of the form. In Thomistic thought, beauty is understood to be one of the

---

13. Phelan, "The Concept of Beauty in St. Thomas Aquinas," in *G. B. Phelan*, 177.
14. Phelan, "The Concept of Beauty in St. Thomas Aquinas," in *G. B. Phelan*, 178.
15. Sevier, *Aquinas on Beauty*, 184.

perfections: beauty, truth, and goodness. These constitute the essence of the One, God, the First Cause, the First Being who is the supreme perfection and from whom all other perfections flow. Accordingly, everything that is, everything that has being, not only reflects God but participates in God. Everything that participates in being participates in the beautiful.

In the *Commentary on the Divine Names*, Aquinas speaks of the beauty of God and the beauty found in all creation. God is the First Good; he is *supersubstantiale pulchrum*—supersubstantially beautiful, beautiful beyond being. He is *pulcherrimus et superpulcher*; as Eco translates this section of the text, God is "beautiful in himself and not in respect of anything else."[16] The beauty in creation, the beauty in humanity, is the result of its "participation in the first cause, which makes all things beautiful . . . *pulchritudo autem participatio primae causae quae omnia pulchra facit*."[17] Whereas God is beautiful in himself and not in respect of anything else, the beauty of creation and the beautiful that is the product of the human imagination does not stand by itself. To partake of, to participate in beauty is to participate in being; and all being, everything that is, participates in God.

This raises the question what it means to "participate in" the beautiful or to participate in the First Cause. Aquinas takes the language or image of "participating in" from Plato, who used it as a means of explaining the relation between universals and particulars. Particulars exist in space and time and are instances of universals. The one is an archetype and the other an imitation or an imperfect instance of the archetype or universal. In speaking of the relation of the particular to the universal, Plato says that the particular participates in the universal. But what does it mean for a particular, which exists in space and time, to participate in a universal, which is timeless and has no existence in this world? Hospers argues that the explanation offered by Plato concerning the relation between particulars and universals "cannot be literally, or even similar to, any of the situations that Plato presents."[18] Accordingly, Hospers offers a revised formulation, which he suggests Plato hints at but never fully articulates. In this formulation, x (a particular) participates in y (a universal), which is to say that x exemplifies or is an instance of y. Perfect goodness, perfect justice, perfect beauty—as universals, these have no perfect instances in this world; however, there are imperfect instances or imperfect exemplifications of these.

16. Eco, *Aesthetics of Thomas Aquinas*, 27–28.
17. Eco, *Aesthetics of Thomas Aquinas*, 27.
18. Hospers, *Introduction to Philosophical Analysis*, 356–57.

While idea of exemplification is useful as a place to begin to grasp the idea of a universal quality made tangible in the world as an imperfect instance, the substance, the reality, of created beauty, its breadth and depth as an objective property, must not be minimized. Aquinas argues that the beauty found in humanity, in each human creature, is not merely a reflection of the divine but is rather something that is in itself beautiful. This is so precisely because God has ascribed to humanity this quality. To return to Eco's summary of Aquinas on this point, Eco says: "Everything is beautiful and comes together in beauty; everything is constructed in accordance with beauty; everything shines with beauty and declares and manifests beauty, the order which the creator Good has assigned to things—the combining of parts, their unifying communion, their harmony—constitutes the rationale of being, goodness, and beauty."[19]

This notwithstanding, there is a measure of reserve in Aquinas concerning the beauty of created things. In *The Divine Names*, Aquinas emphasizes the fact that the beauty of God (according to the reading of Maritain) "is without alteration or vicissitude without increase or diminution." This he contrasts with created beauty, the beauty of things, "which have all a particularised beauty,"[20] and to which he attaches the notable caveat that "the beauty of the creature is nothing but a similitude of the divine beauty shared among things."[21] Maritain interprets this accordingly: "Analogous concepts (by which he means transcendentals) are properly predicable only of God, in whom the perfection they describe exists in a 'formal-eminent' manner, in a pure and infinite state." By contrast, "they are to be found *in things* only as a scattered and prismatised reflection of the face of God."[22] Eco agrees. After citing Aquinas's reference to the beautiful and beauty being "distinguished with respect to participation and participants,"[23] Eco reaffirms Aquinas's commitment to the theological truth that "in God there is no defect. In Him, beauty is not present in one part rather than in another, nor is it present under some particular aspect. Rather, God is

---

19. Eco, *Aesthetics of Thomas Aquinas*, 29.

20. Maritain, *Art and Scholasticism*, 25. Maritain reviews the thought of Aquinas found in *De Divinis Nominibus*, cap. 4, lessons 5 and 6.

21. Aquinas, *De Divinis Nominibus*, lect. 5, as cited in Maritain, *Art and Scholasticism*, 25.

22. Maritain, *Art and Scholasticism*, 24; emphasis added.

23. Eco, *Aesthetics of Thomas Aquinas*, 27.

beautiful simply and in all respects."[24] By contrast, humankind is beautiful because of its relationship to the First Good. And yet, Eco takes pains to make it clear that, according to Aquinas, the beauty we find in things is not a "mere reflection" of the character of God as beautiful and good but the consequence of "participation in a . . . beauty which is identified with the First Good and therefore with Being."[25] And so, we are to understand the beauty of humankind and the created order as less than the perfect beauty and truth of God and yet more than a mere reflection of his glory.

The proclamation that humankind is formed in the very image of God is recorded in the Genesis text: "Then God said, 'Let us make mankind in our image, according to our likeness' . . . . So, God created humankind in his image, in the image of God he created them; male and female he created them" (Gen 1:26–27). By implication, all of humanity, indeed, all created things, are worthy in and of themselves by virtue of God's action; and while it is beyond the scope of this volume and my own capacity to fully interrogate the depths of what it means to be created in God's image, it is no more than a modest beginning to recognize and affirm that to be created in the image of God is to possess the capacity to see and value the beautiful and the good, to be capable of willing and doing the good and creating the beautiful. And yet, in the mind of Aquinas, not creating but rather *composing* the beautiful. For only God has the power to create, that is, to make something out of nothing. Our work as his creation is to form the beautiful out of preexistent materials, to compose something out of that which is already given.

The beauty of God, then, is evidenced in creation—the physical world and humanity created in God's image. Carol Harrison, in her volume *Beauty and Revelation in the Thought of Saint Augustine*, says: "Creation, therefore, like Scripture, assumes the nature of a book, witnessing to its author: like Scripture and the Incarnation of the Word of God, it contains and engenders symbols, allegories, and, indeed, sacraments, which enable its invisible, spiritual sense—its Creator—to be seen more clearly through and in the visible."[26] She could have spoken in the same terms of Aquinas, for both would have based the same claim for divine revelation through creation on Saint Paul's argument in the Letter to the Romans: "Ever since the creation of the world his eternal power and divine nature, invisible

---

24. Eco, *Aesthetics of Thomas Aquinas*, 28.
25. Eco, *Aesthetics of Thomas Aquinas*, 27.
26. Harrison, *Beauty and Revelation*, 120.

though they are, have been understood and seen through the things he has made" (Rom 1:20). Harrison tells us that Augustine, in the final book of *De Trinitate*, quotes from the Book of Wisdom: "Let them know how much better the Lord of them is for the first Author of Beauty hath created them.... For by the greatness and beauty of the creatures, proportionably the Maker of them is seen."[27] So, the beauty of God is evidenced in creation and its creatures. But it is also evidenced in the splendor of the works of his creatures, in the products of the human imagination, such as mathematics, poetry, music, and painting. These works constitute worlds we are able to inhabit, worlds that lead us to that which is part of and yet extends beyond the ordinary and commonplace of our experience; worlds that elicit responses of wonder and admiration that are spontaneous, or that are slow-growing and emerge instead out of a patient and focused attention, out of discipline of the mind and the senses.

As we consider what it is to give patient and focused attention to signs or more specifically evidences of God in the beautiful, we approach the subject of the contemplation of the beautiful. For Aquinas, contemplation, along with other rational capacities of mind, establishes the primacy of human beings over other parts of the created order. Where in contemplation of the beautiful there is recognition of its divine source, there is also contemplation of God. Such contemplation leads to a vital union with the object of contemplation and to participation in the presence of God. This leads us from the philosophical to the theological, to which we shall turn in the final section of this chapter. At present, however, we look to the nature of beauty and its relation to pleasure and happiness.

BEAUTY, PLEASURE, AND HAPPINESS

According to the ancients and medievals, beauty was defined not only in terms of its relation to the good but also in its relation to pleasure and happiness; that is, beauty was understood to produce pleasure in those who participate in it, and this pleasure led to happiness. Plato spoke of "pure" pleasure, altogether devoid of pain. This is the pleasure he associated with the experience of the beautiful. Aristotle proposed a more psychologically complex view, arguing that the pleasure taken in the beautiful involved a contemplative exploration of human feeling; for example, in the context of observing a tragic drama, we experience the quality of fear and pity and

27. Book of Wisdom 13: 1–5, as cited in Harrison, *Beauty and Revelation*, 122.

know them for what they are, without being moved to action as we would be in the ordinary course of life. In his view, the pleasure taken in the beautiful is linked to knowledge of human emotion.

Aquinas makes the point that among God's creatures, only humankind delights in beauty for its own sake ("*solus homo delectatur in ipsa pulchritudine sensibilium secundum seipsam*").[28] This, of course, is the consequence of humanity's unique capacity for thought, reflection, and contemplation. Of God's creatures, humankind alone takes pleasure in the beautiful for its own sake, because this pleasure is derived from contemplation of the beautiful and not merely the pleasure taken in sensual experience. Accordingly, Aquinas, like Aristotle,[29] viewed the pleasure taken in the contemplation of the beautiful as distinct from that pertaining to the preservation of the species ("*ista delectation non pertinent ad conservationem naturae*"); that is, such pleasures were unconnected with activities of the flesh and therefore not in need of temperance.

With respect to the emotional outcomes of participation in the beautiful, the affective consequences are often mingled and certainly not limited to joy and delight. Nonetheless, joy and delight are important features of the pleasure we take in response to the beautiful, and, at some points, this joy is akin to the experience of religious ecstasy. For the Greeks, the term *ecstasy* had a literal meaning of being displaced and came to be understood as a form of distraction, the result of an emotion such as fear, astonishment, or terror. In the sixteenth century, Erasmus used the term to invoke the notion of rapture, where one is transported out of oneself. Erasmus also captures the connotations of transportment and distraction in the phrase *mentis error*, which refers to "a certain joyful wandering of the mind."[30] This wandering of the mind was understood to constitute a striving away from the body to a place of contentment with God. It was not perceived as an escape from or abdication of responsibility but as an activity of a higher order than everyday experience. For Erasmus, this blissful state was a "premium" or reward gained as a consequence of seeking and attaining union with God. Religious ecstasy was understood to offer a vision of the divine and a glimpse of eternal bliss. Here, one finds a theme common to Aristotle

---

28. Aquinas, *Summa Theologiae* 1, Q91, A3, ad. 3.

29. Aristotle, in *Eudemian Ethics* (1230b), argues that attending to the beautiful in a manner of contemplation is not to be considered intemperate. See also Hanfling, *Philosophical Aesthetics*, 117–19.

30. Erasmus, *Praise of Folly*, as cited by Screech, *Ecstasy*, 131.

and Aquinas: contemplation of the beautiful is understood to be a dynamic mental process by which one seeks a union, a vital union, with the beautiful. This union is contemplative and marked by its cognitive nature—a contemplation that involves a seeing informed by reason and information, a seeing not to be confused with mere looking. Apprehension of the beautiful is also often marked by a timelessness, a distraction and transportation to which Erasmus refers with respect to religious ecstasy, the sense of being removed from the world about us.

Finally, there is also a reward in consequence of the contemplation of the beautiful, as there is in the contemplation of God—a reward that is sometimes the experience of delight and sometimes ecstasy. In our experience of the beautiful, we at times experience what the playwright Terence refers to as being "anointed with joy" (*delibitum gaudio*).[31] Such joy is rare in human experience. It is part of that which contributes to the good life and part of that which is specifically human. If the contemplation of art and engagement with the beautiful results in pleasure and delight, it also contributes to happiness. As Aquinas argues, participation in the good contributes to happiness; accordingly, participation in the beautiful contributes to happiness, for beauty is a mode of goodness.

It is clear that Aquinas views the contemplation of the beautiful as significant not merely because it provides pleasure but because it leads to happiness, and happiness is found in returning to the Source, in knowing God. Contemplation of the beautiful leads to happiness because it is a means by which we are able to participate in, partake of, that First Cause; it is a means of communing with God, not because God is in some sense in the object, but because the beautiful reflects the beauty of God and is itself a grace of God. This, I take to be a salient feature of Aquinas's thought and one of the principal notions that accounts for the importance of the aesthetic in the Christian life.

Beauty: The Shift to Subjectivist Accounts

The view of the ancients and medievals concerning the status of beauty as an objective reality persisted until the mid-eighteenth century. With David Hume's *Of the Standard of Taste* (1757) and Kant's *Critique of Judgment* (1790), a profound shift occurred in the philosophical landscape regarding the idea of the beautiful. Both Hume and Kant repositioned beauty as

---

31. The verb *gaudeo* means to rejoice, be glad, take pleasure in, delight in.

dependent upon taste and the response of the percipient. Hume understood beauty not as a quality of things but as a "sentiment," which is to be understood as a "reflective impression." This technical language of sentiment is clarified for us by Theodore Gracyk, who notes that the reflective impressions of which Hume speaks "are not impressions of the senses," but "responses to sensory impressions."[32] However, this aesthetic subjectivism leaves the field open to mere relativism, such that what may be beautiful for one may not be beautiful for another. But Hume objects to such relativism. Proper judgments of a work's "universal" aesthetic value are possible, in his view, but often require the adjudication of "true" critics, those with "strong sense, united to delicate sentiment, improved by practice, perfected by comparison, and cleared of all prejudice."[33]

Kant, in his *Critique of Judgment*, also makes the claim that beauty is ultimately a matter of taste and therefore subjective: "The judgment of taste, therefore, is not a cognitive judgment, and so not logical, but aesthetic—which means that it is one whose determining ground *cannot be other than subjective*."[34] So then, both Hume and Kant argue that beauty is a matter of taste and that there exist no criteria or ultimate standard for taste; and yet, both take pains to argue that not any taste will do, for there is both good taste and poor taste. Hence, both argue the need of qualified and appropriate judges or critics to render judgments of taste that are appropriate. As Sartwell puts it, Kant and Hume both "treat judgments of beauty neither precisely as purely subjective nor precisely as objective but, as we might put it, as inter-subjective."[35] Despite their claims for universally valid judgments that would protect the idea of the beautiful from claims that beauty was little more than a term of approbation, the general disposition to the idea of beauty had altered. The positions of both Kant and Hume were thoroughly secular and fundamentally subjectivist, and without the anchor of the transcendentals as absolute qualities of being, without reference to God and the created order, the concept of beauty was soon pushed to the side in favor of an individualistic and subjective reading of aesthetic experience.

As an aside, it must be said that the role of perception in relation to the beautiful was commonly discussed in the Middle Ages. While Augustine and Aquinas took an objectivist position, there was a greater measure

---

32. Gracyk, "Hume's Aesthetics."
33. Hume, *Philosophical Works*, 3:278.
34. Kant, *Critique of Judgment*, 41.
35. Sartwell, "Beauty."

of ambivalence in the thought of Richard of St. Victor, Bonaventure, William of Auvergne, and Witelo, each of whom took account of the knowing subject and object perceived.[36] Even Aquinas, in his *Summa*, inserts at one point the phrase "*pulchra enim dicuntur quae visa placent*" (beautiful things are those that please when seen).[37] The medievals were undeniably cognizant that beauty existed for a purpose and not for its own sake. It existed for the greater glory of the God whose beauty it reflected, and it existed for the pleasure and benefit of humankind.

As noted previously, by the turn of the twentieth century, there was little interest in the view that beauty exists as an objective phenomenon, as real as matter or energy, as Hunter Mead once put it. One of the last serious philosophical conributions to the theory of beauty in which the object remains the focus of attention was offered by the British philosopher C. E. Moore. In an essay entitled "The Refutation of Idealism," Moore argues against Berkeley's assumption of the synonymity of the terms "being" and "being perceived" and sets forth one of the principles of his mature philosophical work, the tenet that objects exist distinct from acts of consciousness. Moore's treatment of the question of beauty in the treatise *Principia Ethica* (1903) takes the beautiful object as something in existence and something that exists independent of consciousness. However, it is his contention that there can be no criterion of beauty. "All that can be true," he suggests, "is that certain objects are beautiful, *because* they have certain characteristics, in the sense that they would not be beautiful *unless* they had them."[38]

Apart from the few, like Moore, the European philosophical community after Kant moved to a subjectivist view of beauty. As Crispin Sartwell argues, "The twentieth century . . . abandoned beauty as the dominant goal of the arts . . . in part, because its trivialization in theory led artists to believe that they ought to pursue more real and more serious projects." In the same essay, Sartwell put the matter this way: "If beauty is a subjective pleasure, it would seem to have no higher status than anything that entertains, amuses, or distracts; it seems odd or ridiculous to regard it as being comparable in importance to truth or justice, for example."[39] But this shift

---

36. See the discussion of "The Function and Nature of the Aesthetic *Visio*" in Eco, *Aesthetic of Thomas Aquinas*, 49–63.

37. Aquinas, *Summa Theologiae* 1, Q5, A4, ad. 1.

38. Moore, *Principia Ethica*, 202.

39. Sartwell, "Beauty."

from an objectivist to a subjectivist view was accompanied by a secularism that also rejected the linkage of the beautiful with the good, and the beautiful and the good as qualities of God, the source of all beauty and goodness. The recovery of beauty, and the reassertion of its significance as a mode of goodness, tied both to being and the character of God, has been undertaken by a number of theologians in the twenty-first century. We return to the matter of beauty, being, and the Christian life at the conclusion of this essay. For the moment, we turn to the problem of how the beautiful is to be identified.

BEAUTY THEORY AND THE SIGNIFICANCE OF CRITICISM

Beauty theory raises many problems, of course, including the problem concerning the relation between beauty and the object that possesses it, and the question of whether there are identifiable necessary or sufficient conditions of beauty. In this context, I do not intend to address the first question to any extent, apart from offering a simple clarification. There are two principal views of the relationship between beauty and the object that possesses it: the transcendental view (Plato) and the naturalistic view (Aquinas, for example). The first view argues that beauty is a universal quality that exists independent and outside of the object and supervenes on the object by virtue of its formal quality, while the second view holds that beauty emerges from the work as a quality and characteristic of the work. Of greater interest in this context is the problem of how beauty is identified. So let us turn, then, to the question of whether it is possible to establish a criterion of the beautiful or to provide a list of necessary or sufficient conditions such that where these conditions are met, we may agree that the object is, in fact, beautiful.

In response, we must say that philosophers are, in this age, unable to agree upon a criterion of what constitutes the beautiful, or what is now called aesthetic value. This dilemma reflects the more fundamental disagreement concerning the concept of art and the question of what constitutes art. To Plotinus, and Plato before him, the beauty of material things was the result of participation in ideal-form. Beauty was the result of form, of unity and coherence. For Aquinas, this fundamental concept of the relation of beauty to form remained. However, the concepts of unity in variety, coherence, integrity, consonance, and clarity have not satisfied modern critics. In fact, it has been precisely the inability of philosophers to generate an acceptable set of conditions of beauty that has led to the large-scale rejection of any objectivist theory and a general inclination toward subjectivist interpretations of beauty as a product of mind. Moore, who supports the notion of beauty as objective reality, claims that there is "no single criterion of beauty." "All that can be true," he suggests, "is that certain objects are beautiful, 'because' they have certain characteristics, in the sense that they would not be beautiful 'unless' they had them."[40] If Moore is correct and there can be no single criterion of the beautiful, the question remains, how shall we identify the beautiful?

It must be admitted that the classical conditions such as unity in variety and the criteria of clarity, integrity, and proportion laid down by Aquinas are not adequate of themselves for the assessment of beauty in the twentieth century. In fact, whether applied in this century or another, these criteria may tell us little, for an object may be perfectly proportioned and yet visually or aurally tedious; it may possess the qualities of unity and coherence and yet be imaginatively banal. But lest we despair of finding any way forward, it is worth noting that this task poses difficulties no greater than those presented by the concepts of truth and knowledge, for neither is there agreement concerning the nature of truth or whether it is possible to know with certainty anything at all. Yet we accept the necessity of these concepts in our way of thinking about the world and about human experience. In response to the problem of whether it is possible to know God, Erasmus suggests suspension of judgment and acceptance of the institutional, that is to say, Catholic view. Doubt concerning ultimate religious knowledge was, in Erasmus's view, best addressed by accepting the judgment of those in a position of knowledge and authority, the pope and fathers of the church, as well as the traditions of Christianity. Recourse to tradition and authority as a strategy for identifying truth or establishing a vision of the future has largely fallen from favor in modern Western culture.

With respect to the formation of artistic judgments, the argument for reliance upon authority or acceptance of an institutional view is an eminently sensible proposition. For, in fact, we routinely rely upon the authoritative judgment of others in our common experience. Let us take as an example the diagnosis and treatment of a medical problem. Here, we turn to a physician; indeed, if the problem is acute, we turn to a medical specialist rather than a general practitioner, on the assumption that a more detailed knowledge of the subject is vital to a correct diagnosis and appropriate

---

40. Moore, *Principia Ethica*, 202.

treatment of the problem. In fact, we routinely accept the claim to authority that comes of knowledge, training, and the benefit of a received tradition, whether it concerns repairing an engine, settling a will, or even selecting an over-the-counter drug. With respect to the problem of beauty or aesthetic value (we use the terms interchangeably here) and the adjudication of experts, there are, admittedly, problems to be addressed, including what constitutes an expert, and the problem presented by conflicting judgments of experts (for whatever collection of musical experts are identified, their judgments concerning the comparative merits of musical works shall most certainly produce as much controversy as consensus). Nonetheless, acceptance of the counsel of authorities concerning that which constitutes the beautiful in music and the other arts seems a reasonable point of departure, despite the reservations we may hold concerning disagreement respecting particular artistic judgments.

As a second path, and one which can be used in conjunction with the first, I suggest we turn to an argument posed by C. S. Lewis. According to this view, a determination of the beautiful or the aesthetically valuable[41] would take into account any work that causes even the naïve listener, reader, or observer to "surrender," to receive a work in a way such that the self is put to the side.[42] In Lewis's view, where there is evidence of authentic engagement with the work, there ought be the assumption of literary value, for the mode of reception suggests that the object of attention is capable of eliciting the rewards of engagement with works of literary value—that is, delight, pleasure, happiness, joy. I do not say, neither does Lewis suggest, that there exists an "aesthetic" emotion distinct from all other emotional experience and that it is this which is common to the experience of art. Rather, it is the joy, delight, and (sometimes) ecstasy that the work evokes that constitutes evidence of engagement with the beautiful, with what Lewis terms the artist's "sensuous and intellectual invention."[43] The role of the critic or expert is to point to the beautiful, to identify that which is of value, so that we may benefit from their labor and expertise rather than suffer the consequences of poor choices made in ignorance. As our acceptance of the judgment of a physician is in some measure contingent upon the level of satisfaction we find in that judgment—should the physician's diagnosis

---

41. Lewis does not use this phrase; for in speaking of literature, he refers to literary value.

42. Lewis, *Experiment in Criticism*, 14–26.

43. Lewis, *Experiment in Criticism*, 24.

lead to a satisfactory treatment of my ailment, I consider this good reason to continue to trust his or her medical judgment—judgments of artistic value, to some extent at least, are assessed in terms of whether or not they lead to the experience of beauty and the rewards of participation in the beautiful. But the role of the expert extends beyond merely identifying that which is of value. The claim of the work of artistic substance on the reader, on the listener, is not only that we behold it but that we explore its imaginative richness. The role of the expert involves guiding the percipient into a fuller appreciation and understanding of the compositional complexities of the work.

Regardless of the various historical views that offered a theory of beauty as an objective property, the dominant position in the contemporary world is a subjectivist account of beauty: "It is good because I like it." That is, the work is considered to be beautiful, good, aesthetically valuable, because it elicits certain feelings and, ultimately, the approbation of the observer. Lewis's proposal regarding the identification of works of literary value clearly endorses a substantial reliance upon the individual's experience of the work as a basis for determining whether it possesses literary value. However, to extrapolate from this the suggestion that a work be identified as beautiful on the basis of *any* favorable experience of the work is to misinterpret a central feature of Lewis's argument. Lewis does not suggest that a work has literary value simply because it is liked by one individual or by many. His is not, in fact, a psychological definition, such as that offered above (that is, I like it; therefore, it is good and beautiful). Rather, he suggests that in the absence of a satisfactory criteria for the identification of literary value, we look instead for indicators of participation in the good. That is, we deduce from the nature of the observer's interaction with the object that the object is of literary value. This is not merely to say that the beautiful is that which offers emotional gratification. Lewis recommends consideration of the particular character of the literary experience. The literary response, he says, is characterized by one's surrender to the work, the demand of the work upon the mind and senses, and the capacity of the work to sustain its claim upon the reader. Here, the argument shifts implicitly to the objective qualities of the work, for the basis of determining whether the work is one of artistic value does not rest on the work being "favorably" received or the work offering a measure of amusement or entertainment; it rests on the assumption that the enduring surrender of the mind and senses is a literary response to the dynamic and compelling quality of the literary work, its construct, its way of being as an object of beauty. The bad or poor work "cannot," he says, "be enjoyed with that full and 'disciplined' reception which the few gives to a good one."[44]

What is proposed here is that the ability to identify and perceive the beautiful and valuable in art is not an inherent human attribute. The beautiful can, quite simply, be missed. We learn to recognize and appreciate the beautiful in music and the other arts, as we do the beautiful in other things. With respect to music, part of the purpose of music education, whether in conservatories, public schools, or universities, is precisely to enable individuals to participate in that which is musically good, to recognize and appreciate the beautiful in music, to make independent judgments of taste based upon a knowledge of musical works. This is also the case for literature, poetry, and the other arts. In this educative process, we rely on the expertise and judgments of others. I suggest that rather than seeking a definition of the beautiful and, more specifically, a definition of the beautiful in the arts, we seek the guidance of the artistic masters and experts. Given the idea of beauty as something excellent and worthy as an object of its kind, the significance of criticism in the determination of value becomes obvious. The judgment of specialists—composers, performers, and learned critics—is essential in the determination of what constitutes the beautiful in music. Thereafter, we shall expect our experience of the beautiful to provide the promised reward of pleasure and delight, the reward of being enveloped in the world of the work. These pleasures are perhaps the most reliable witness to the beautiful.

THE RECLAMATION OF BEAUTY: BALTHASAR, VILADESAU, AND GARCIA-RIVERA

In 2009, Hans Urs von Balthasar, a Swiss theologian and Catholic priest, published the first of seven volumes entitled *The Glory of the Lord*, in which he sets about the task of reclaiming the idea of beauty as a divine quality, "a word from which religion, and theology in particular, have taken their leave and distanced themselves in modern times."[45] In the words of the Balthasar scholar Aidan Nichols, Balthasar lamented the reduction of beauty to "a merely this-worldly aesthetics." He interprets Balthasar's concern this way: "The notion of the sheer beauty of the divine Being has

---

44. Lewis, *Experiment in Criticism*, 20.
45. Balthasar, *Seeing the Form*, 17.

disappeared. The severance of beauty from goodness and truth also helps to explain the perceived reduction of the moral order to a self-centered relativism, and the retrenchment of the metaphysical order to a materialism placed at the service of either technology or psychology or both. The final upshot of all this, he predicts, will be the incapacity for either faith or love."[46] In Balthasar's thought, like the Scholastics and ancients before him, beauty is necessarily connected with the good and the true. He speaks of beauty as that which "dances as an uncontained splendour around the double constellation of the true and the good and their inseparable relation to one another."[47] Moreover, beauty is not merely a matter of appearance; rather, it is tied to "logical and ethical concepts, concepts of truth and value." It is tied to what he identifies as "a comprehensive doctrine of Being." The beautiful is that which illuminates "the real presence of the depths, of the whole of reality, *and* it is a real pointing beyond itself to these depths."[48] Drawing on the tradition of St. Thomas Aquinas and "a participation metaphysic of the sort St. Thomas used increasingly in his work,"[49] Balthasar speaks of the Christian life as a form, the form that shapes the Christian, "the form that surrounds him inexorably like a coat of armour and which nonetheless is the very thing that bestows suppleness on him and which makes him free of all uncertainty and all paralyzing fears, free for himself and his highest possibilities."[50] It is this body of thought from which theology (and, less surprisingly, philosophy) has turned in much of the past century or more that Balthasar wishes to reclaim.

Richard Viladesau, in *Theological Aesthetics: God in Imagination, Beauty, and Art*, joins Balthasar in asserting that theology's appropriation of the research methods of the sciences has been accompanied by a neglect of and turning away from beauty. Mirroring Balthasar on this matter, Viladesau argues that having "neglected beauty as an object of inquiry," theology has also "largely lost its connection with living religion and spirituality."[51] Again in concert with Balthasar, Viladesau says, "The academic world largely reflects this ideal of abstract, objectivizing rationalism;

---

46. Nichols, *Key to Balthasar*, 12. Here he refers to Balthasar's *Glory of the Lord*, 1:18–19.

47. Balthasar, *Glory of the Lord*, 1:18.

48. Balthasar, *Glory of the Lord*, 1:118.

49. Nichols, *Key to Balthasar*, 3.

50. Balthasar, *Glory of the Lord*, 1:23–24.

51. Viladesau, *Theological Aesthetics*, 12.

and academic theology has to a large degree allowed itself to be seduced by it." Consequently, Viladesau adds, "it stands in danger of losing its inherent spirituality, and with it its inherent poetry and beauty." Viladesau further develops the argument, drawing upon Karl Rahner, who argues for a return to an aesthetic dimension to theology. Specifically, Rahner argues the lack of what he calls a "mystagogical and poetic" theology. Again, in Viladesau's words, this means "not only that theology should take account of feeling, beauty, and art as aspects of religion and of primary religious language, but also that theology itself should speak 'with feeling' and in images, integrating the religious and poetic elements into its mode of discourse."[52]

This is to say that, insamuch as the central task of theology is to lead to "an existential encounter with God,"[53] the work of theology is not adequately served or appropriately constrained by the parameters of an "exact science."[54] Rahner reminds us of the place of mystery and ineffable faith in the life of the Christian church: "God, and what is meant by God, can only be grasped when we surrender our own conceptual understanding to the ineffable and holy mystery which lays hold on us as the mystery which is near to us, and which embraces us in love."[55]

The work of reclaiming the concept of beauty for the church has been the project of many, in addition to the theologians referenced above, including John Navone, Patrick Sherry, Frank Burch Brown, and Gerard van der Leeuw, among many others. But I conclude this section by directing the reader to the work of Alejandro Garcia-Rivera, an American theologian who writes out of a Hispanic tradition. Garcia-Rivera follows in the tradition of the Greeks and the church fathers when he asserts that "Beauty's origin . . . is divine. Beauty's origin is God himself."[56] Having taken the position of affirming the objective nature of beauty and claiming for beauty the status of a transcendental, along with unity, goodness, and truth, Garcia-Rivera moves the discourse in a different direction. Before outlining this new direction for theological aesthetics, he begins with a summary of the historical problem we have explored in this chapter, citing Ernest Cassirer, who speaks of the antagonism in philosophical aesthetics in these terms:

---

52. Viladesau, *Theological Aesthetics*, 12.

53. Viladesau, *Theological Aesthetics*, 13.

54. Viladesau, *Theological Aesthetics*, 12.

55. Rahner, "A Theology That We Can Live With," as cited in Viladesau, *Theological Aesthetics*, 13.

56. Garcia-Rivera, *Community of the Beautiful*, 14.

"Language and art are constantly oscillating between opposite poles, an objective and a subjective pole."[57] Cassirer proceeds to narrate the shift in philosophical perspective in this manner: "Before the eighteenth century, the objective pole dominated and art was seen as mimesis, or imitative. In other words, Beauty was thoroughly objective.... When Kant appeared on the scene... philosophical aesthetics decidedly shifted from an emphasis on the objectivity of Beauty to its subjective reception (and creation) as the beautiful. In terms of philosophical categories this meant a shift in emphasis from an objective metaphysics of Beauty to the transcendental analysis of the subjective or intersubjective process which accounts for Beauty's reception within human experience."[58] Garcia-Rivera argues that theological aesthetics ought not ignore classicist thought found in the metaphysics of beauty; but neither should it "reject the great insights of Modernity into the dynamism of the human spirit which is, after all, the receptor of Beauty."[59]

Garcia-Rivera asserts that the task of theological aesthetics is to address "this modern theological crisis by doing justice to these twin aspects of Beauty: its absolute origins in the transcendent God who nonetheless wishes to be known and loved by his human creation." "Theological aesthetics," he says, "attempts to make clear once again the connection between Beauty and the beautiful, between Beauty's divine origins and its appropriation by the human heart."[60] And so he asks, "What is Beauty if it is not received?"[61] And, "Do we believe in a God who wishes to be known and loved by his human creation? Does the human creature, in turn, have the capacity to know and love this God?"[62]

It is here that Garcia-Rivera introduces into his theological aesthetics the categories of glory and praise. Beautiful form, the origin of which is divine, glorifies God and elicits from the people of God praise. As its counterpoint, the category of praise addresses the subjectivity of beauty. For Garcia-Rivera, "Theological aesthetics recognizes both that the divine abyss is meant to be crossed and that the pure Gift is meant to be appropriated by the human heart."[63] Garcia-Rivera concludes by asserting that "the

---

57. Ernest Cassirer, as quoted in Garcia-Rivera, *Community of the Beautiful*, 12.
58. Ernest Cassirer, as quoted in Garcia-Rivera, *Community of the Beautiful*, 12–13.
59. Garcia-Rivera, *Community of the Beautiful*, 14.
60. Garcia-Rivera, *Community of the Beautiful*, 11.
61. Garcia-Rivera, *Community of the Beautiful*, 10.
62. Garcia-Rivera, *Community of the Beautiful*, 11.
63. Garcia-Rivera, *Community of the Beautiful*, 20.

two fundamental dimensions to Beauty are Beauty's issuing forth and the movement of the human heart giving thanks for Beauty on behalf of all creation."[64] As Garcia-Rivera works out a theological aesthetics, he formulates the view that "the work of the people," that is, *leit-ourgos* or liturgy, "may be seen as the human art which receives Glory and returns Praise."[65] Of particular note is Rivera's declaration, in line with the theology of Teilhard concerning the work of the believer, that this liturgy, this work of the people, "is an act whose boundaries go far beyond the church walls." He sees this as an "aesthetics of human work" and a theological aesthetics of human art. This response to beauty, both the beauty of nature and the beauty of human art, is, in his mind, "above all, a giving of thanks," of praise.[66]

In this theology of gift and thanks, Rivera makes the point that as the beautiful, the gift, is original, so is praise. Praise, he says, "is original thanks for it rises forth out of the context of human freedom and so it is given fresh and new from the depths of the original freedom of the human heart."[67] "God's Beauty may issue forth as Glory," he says, " . . . but does not find completion until it ends in creation's praise."[68] Here is a triadic relationship that gathers together the object of glory, the human spirit that receives it, and the response of thanks and praise to God, the giver of gifts to his creation.

I conclude this brief look at Garcia-River with a recapitulation of his assertion that "the two fundamental dimensions to Beauty are Beauty's issuing forth and the movement of the human heart giving thanks for Beauty on behalf of all creation."[69] The emergence of the beautiful, standing as an objective reality in the world, and its reception by the percipient recognizing the beauty and goodness of the work together constitute an amalgam of the objective and subjective and an overcoming of the historical polarity that has shaped so much of the discourse concerning the nature of beauty. But then, it is more than this. For as Garcia-Rivera reminds us, the response of the faithful is not merely to respond to the work in recognition of the beauty found there but to be thankful and to give praise to God as the source of all that is beautiful, good, and true.

64. Garcia-Rivera, *Community of the Beautiful*, 20.
65. Garcia-Rivera, *Community of the Beautiful*, 17.
66. Garcia-Rivera, *Community of the Beautiful*, 18.
67. Garcia-Rivera, *Community of the Beautiful*, 19.
68. Garcia-Rivera, *Community of the Beautiful*, 20.
69. Garcia-Rivera, *Community of the Beautiful*, 20.

NOTES FOR THE CHURCH

This chapter is based on the concept that to participate in the beautiful, that is, to create or contemplate the beautiful, is to participate in the First Cause; and that participation in the beautiful is one of the ways in which it is possible to encounter and know God. As Christians, we recognize the fact of this confluence of the spiritual and the aesthetic from our personal experience. In the contemplation and reflective experience of natural beauty, we discover not only a heightened use of the senses and an intensification of experience elicited by the dynamic quality of the beauty of nature, but a sense that God is present in his creation. This is also true of our experience of artworks. The sheer sensual quality and form of the work excites the human senses and imagination and provokes the pleasure taken in the beautiful. It is the beauty of the work, its presentational quality, of which I speak, and the capacity of this quality to lead us to God. Here, we encounter the particular pleasure that results in a measure of happiness; here, we encounter a grace of God; here, we may encounter the presence of God.

Aquinas contends that happiness is an end that all humankind seeks; and though, in his view, perfect happiness cannot in this life be attained, given the transitory nature of life, the presence of evil in the world, and the fact that perfect happiness occurs only in union with God,[70] it may, he suggests, be partially realized in this life. Indeed, the experience of such happiness offers a foretaste of the perfect happiness of eternity. It is the experience of happiness through participation in the beautiful, among other things, that contributes to increased fullness of being. The delight that accompanies the apprehension of beauty is a token of that fact—a token of a fulfilled desire, where the desire is good, because the object of desire is beautiful and therefore worthy of our attention.

Jean Porter, in *The Recovery of Virtue*, speaks of a number of human goods: human life, knowledge and aesthetic appreciation, skilled performances of all kinds, self-integration, authenticity, practical reasonableness, justice and friendship, and religion and holiness.[71] There is much to recommend this list to the Christian church and to each of us who seeks a life of greater faithfulness, obedience, and intimacy with God. In this volume, we attend to the beautiful as both a gift of God present in creation and the products of the human imagination. The latter constitute what Porter

---

70. Aquinas, *Summa Theologiae* 1–2, Q3, A3, co.; 1–2, Q5, A3, co.
71. Porter, *Recovery of Virtue*, 18.

classifies as "skilled performances," for the composition of a painting, a poem, or musical work surely comprise a mode of performance. Moreover, we have spoken of our aesthetic engagement with the beautiful, our perception and reception of beautiful things. Porter quite appropriately links aesthetic appreciation and knowledge, for the former leads to some measure of the latter, a greater knowledge of the beauty observed, and, sometimes, a greater knowledge of God, who at times and places reveals himself in and through the beautiful. Indeed, these are good things, which contribute to an increased fullness and wholeness in our human experience.

Garcia-Rivera suggests that the experience of pleasure and happiness as a consequence of an experience of the beautiful is not the lone objective. Our experience of the beautiful, as Garcia-Rivera reminds us, is found in the praise that follows glory. That is, the experience of glory demands a response. As the people of God, we are reminded of the biblical text to "love the LORD your God with all your heart, and with all your soul, and with all your might" (Deut 6:5) This is the command that the Jewish people recited as part of their daily liturgy. We fulfil this command in part by giving expression to our gratitude and thanks in praise.

This praise takes many forms. We give praise to the Lord in his sanctuary, as Ps 150 says, through our singing, playing of instruments, and through our prayers. We do this individually and corporately. But we also offer praise to God in our daily living, that is, in the manner in which we live and offer our lives, as St. Paul puts it, as a "living sacrifice" to God. Our lives then become a form, an act of praise. It is in this way that our work, in the view of Teilhard, becomes a sanctified process, a holy engagement directed as praise and thankfulness to God.

This is one of the ways in which we understand the artistic endeavors of the Christian—the creation of works of beauty and of artful practice, both of which point to the Lord of creation. These gifts of the imagination we offer to God as acts of praise and thanksgiving. This, then, is part of the work of the people, part of what Garcia-Rivera sees as a broad understanding of the liturgy of life that is constantly mindful of God as the One who is good, true, and beautiful. The One who desires to be in relation with his creation and his people.

Thanks be to God from whom all blessings flow.

3

Emotion and the Arts

INTRODUCTION

From the time of the ancient Greeks, there has been a great deal of speculation and theorizing concerning the specific nature of the relationship between the various arts and human emotion. In this chapter, we investigate the central tenets of expression and signification theories, both of which hold that the principal significance of art lies in its relation to human emotion. At the conclusion of the chapter, we also briefly consider the matter of self-expression, its relation to expression theory, its relevance to art, and its role in Christian worship.

MUSIC AND EMOTION

The earliest systematic treatment of the relationship between music and emotion is found in the writings of those Greeks who attributed to music the capacity to imitate or represent objects of perception and to represent and evoke emotions by means of particular timbres and melodic and rhythmic structures. The *Pythic nome* (586 BC), an instrumental piece played on the aulos depicting Apollo's fight with the dragon, provides what Lang refers to as "the oldest example of program music."[1] Several hundred years later, Aristotle, in reference to what was then a common assumption regarding music and human emotion, spoke of the capacity of music to imitate and the effects of such imitation on its audience:

1. Lang, *Music in Western Civilization*, 10.

> Even in mere melodies there is an imitation of character, for the musical scales differ essentially from one another, and those who hear them are differently affected by each. Some of them make men sad and grave, like the so-called Mixolydian; others enfeeble the mind.... The same principles apply to rhythms; some have a character of rest, others of motion, and of these latter again, some have a more vulgar, others a nobler motion...[2]

In fact, the Hellenistic view of music and its effects extended beyond the ideas of representation and evocation to include the capacity to effect ethical responses in the hearer. Plato, Aristotle, and Damon of Athens, among others, delineate the relation between particular melodic and rhythmic structures and timbres and their effects on the passions and the moral development of the hearer. In book 3 of the *Republic*, Plato treats the question of imitation, which he takes to be degrading and detrimental to the education of the young and therefore unworthy of a place in the ideal society. The Mixolydian and the Syntonolydian modes were to be banished because they represented lamentation and mourning: "After all, they are no use even to women—if we want them to be good women—let alone to men." The Lydian mode and various Ionian modes were understood to have no place in the republic because of their association with indolence, luxury, and drunkenness.[3] The Dorian and Phrygian modes, on the other hand, were considered useful in the training of young warriors and for encouraging virtues essential to the state.

> I don't know about modes.... Leave me the mode which can most fittingly imitate the voice and accents of a brave man in the time of war, or in any externally imposed crisis. When things go wrong, and he faces death and wounds, or encounters some other danger, in all these situations he holds out to the end in a disciplined and steadfast manner. Plus, another mode for someone engaged in some peaceful, voluntary, freely chosen activity. He might be trying to persuade someone of something, making some request—praying to a god, or giving instructions or advice to a man. Or just the opposite. He might be listening patiently to someone else making a request, or explaining something to him, or trying to get him to change his mind, and on that basis acting as he thinks best—without arrogance, acting prudently and calmly in all these situations, and being content with the outcome. These

---

2. Aristotle, *Politics*, as cited in Russell, *Thinking about Music*, 52.
3. Plato, *Republic*, 88.

two modes, then, one for adversity and one for freely chosen activity, the modes which will best imitate the voices of the prudent and of the brave in failure and success. Leave me those.[4]

With respect to the effects of rhythm, Plato defers to Damon and is content for his part to state the obvious and commonly accepted fact that certain rhythms were expressive of "meanness of spirit, arrogance, madness and other faults of character."[5] The rhythms that, in his view, ought to be retained and encouraged were those that expressed their opposites.

Despite the profound influence of Greek thought on Western civilization, the Greeks' view of the particular correspondences between music and human behaviour and development has been negligible. However, the fundamental notion that there exists an important link between music and human emotions, and that the essential value of musical activity is located in the connection between the two, has remained a dominant theme throughout the history of music and the philosophy of music in Western civilization, though the question of the specific relation between music and the emotions has been a matter of constant debate.

In the sixteenth century, music theorist and composer Gioseffe Zarlino spoke of the function of music to assist in the expression of human emotion; this it did in alliance with text. "In so far as he can, he must take care to accompany each word in such a way that, if it denotes harshness, hardness, cruelty, bitterness, and other things of this sort, the harmony will be similar, that is, somewhat hard and harsh, but so that it does not offend. In the same way, if any word expresses complaint, grief, affliction, sighs, tears, and other things of this sort, the harmony will be full of sadness."[6] In this matter, Zarlino was making a point commonly accepted among European composers of the sixteenth century. For as rhetoric was understood as the art of manipulating and directing the emotions of the audience, composers accepted the task of music to express the emotion of the text and thereby affect the emotion of the listener.

In the seventeenth and eighteenth centuries numerous theorists, including Burmeister (*Musica Autoschediastike*, 1601), Neidhardt (*Beste und leichteste Temperatur des Monochordi*, 1706), and Mattheson (*Das neu-eröffnete Orchestre*, 1713), explored the relation between music and the emotions, specifically the emotive connotations of rhythms, scale

---

4. Plato, *Republic*, 88–89.

5. Plato, *Republic*, 90.

6. Zarlino, "Instituzioni armoniche," 66–67.

structures, musical forms and instruments, and the parallels between music and rhetoric.[7] Such was the popular conviction of the relationship between music and human emotion that, in the mid-nineteenth century, Hanslick published *Vom Musikalisch-Schönen* for the specific purpose of addressing what the author describes as the prevalent and "serious methodological error" applied in the criticism and discussion of music, which, contrary to his more formalist perspective, was concerned "not so much with careful investigation of that which is beautiful in music, but rather with giving an account of the feelings which take possession of us when we hear it."[8] By Hanslick's account, the view that the expression of feeling was central to the purpose and value of music was commonplace in the middle of the nineteenth century and had long been accepted as a foundational principle in musical aesthetics. In support of his claim, Hanslick provides numerous quotations (twenty or more, depending upon the specific edition), which he prefaces with these remarks:

> It seems to us hardly necessary for present purposes to attach the names of their authors to the views which we are here concerned to oppose, since these views are less the flowering of special convictions than the expression of a way of thinking which is generally becoming traditional.[9]

Among the items cited in support of the prevalence of the expressionist view are the following:[10]

- The ultimate purpose of music (the claims of the finest orators notwithstanding) is to arouse all feelings by means of tones and their rhythms alone. J. G. Neidhardt (1706)
- Music is the art of expressing our passions by means of tones, as we do in speech by means of words. Sulzer (1793)
- Music is the art of expressing feelings by means of modulation of sounds. It is the language of emotion. C. F. Michaelis (1800)
- The chief and ultimate purpose of music is the imitation, or rather the arousing, of the passions. W. Heinse (1805)

---

7. Buelow, "Affects."
8. Hanslick, *On the Musically Beautiful*, 1.
9. Hanslick, *On the Musically Beautiful*, 86.
10. Hanslick, *On the Musically Beautiful*, 86–90.

- Music represents feelings. Both in itself and hence also in music, every feeling and every mental state has its own particular sound and rhythm. F. Hand (1837)

As these few references suggest, the body of thought concerning the relation between music and human feeling was constituted of a group of ideas and not reduceable to a single proposition. These ideas included the view that music is capable of evoking and arousing human emotions and passions; that it is a means by which the composer is able to vent his or her personal feelings; that it is a means of self-expression; and, most importantly, that music constitutes a language capable of expressing human emotion and enabling others to experience the emotional world of the composer.

The sentiment linking music to the sphere of human emotions continued throughout the nineteenth century. Hegel, for example, addressed the subject in his "Vorlesungen über die Ästhetik" (1818–1820):

> It is a province which unfolds in expanse the expression of every kind of emotion, and every shade of joyfulness, merriment, jest, caprice, jubilation and laughter of the soul, every gradation of anguish, trouble, melancholy, lament, sorrow, pain, longing and the like, no less than those of reverence, adoration, and love fall within the appropriate limits of its expression.[11]

For Hegel, the purpose and extraordinary value of music as art is to express the range and complexity of emotion.

Wagner also had much to say about the relation of music to human feelings. In his treatise *Opera and Drama*, he addresses the task of the composer-artist who is to give expression to human emotion. To this end, the work of the poet-musician was, in his view, ultimately of greater value than that of the absolute or pure musician; for the poet was able to liberate the musician and enable him to express "undreamt delights of blissful Feeling."[12] This alliance of music and poetry in the service of human emotion harkens back to Zarlino's writings on the subject in the sixteenth century and to the ancients before him, where one encounters the idea of the embodiment of feeling in the work, the evoking of emotion and the arousing of passion in the percipient.

Along with the concept of the arts as a vehicle of expression of emotion, there emerged the popular idea of art as communication. Indeed,

---

11. Hegel, "Vorlesungen über die Asthetik," 2:234.
12. Wagner, *Opera and Drama*, 278.

Schopenhauer, among others, was prepared to claim for music the status of "universal language." "The inexpressible depth of all music," he says, "is due to the fact that it reproduces all the emotions of our innermost being."[13] According to Schopenhauer, not only does music constitute a language capable articulating the most profound emotions, a proposition that has gained a currency which continues in some measure to the present, but this language, as a nonverbal mode of communication, is taken to be universal, that is, unbounded by region, culture, and language. This claim rests on the assumption that music as a symbol system can be interpreted and accessed across cultures and disparate languages and can successfully communicate and articulate the depths of human emotional experience in a manner unique to music.

BEYOND MUSIC: ART AND EMOTION IN THE NINETEENTH CENTURY

In nineteenth-century Europe, the view that expression was the principal intent of all artistic endeavor was widely accepted throughout the artistic community as a whole. That is to say, not only was Hanslick's formalist account decidedly a minority view with respect to the value ascribed to music and musical experience, the broadly accepted view of the value of the arts in general rested on the proposition that the arts were foundationally linked with the expression of human feeling. Among the renowned treatments of the subject is the *Preface to Lyrical Ballads*, in which Wordsworth argues that it is the "the wish of the Poet to bring his feelings near to those of the persons whose feelings he describes, nay, for short spaces of time, perhaps, to let himself slip into an entire delusion, and even confound and identify his own feelings with theirs."[14] He proceeds to make what may now seem a remarkable assertion: "All good poetry," he says, "is the spontaneous overflow of powerful feelings."[15] It must be noted that Wordsworth is not suggesting that the writing of poetry is simply a matter of a venting of emotion; nor does he speak of the arousal in the reader of the emotions expressed by the writer. However, his comment respecting poetry and the "overflow of powerful feelings" makes clear his view that the essential purpose of poetry is intimately connected with the expression of emotion.

13. Schopenhauer, "Welt als Wille," 2:171.
14. Wordsworth, *Preface to Lyrical Ballads*, in *Prefaces*, 191.
15. Wordsworth, *Preface to Lyrical Ballads*, in *Prefaces*, 186.

For Wordsworth, the artful expression of emotion is ultimately linked to the poet's principal intent, which is to give pleasure to the reader. Here, he echoes the classical view of the relationship between beauty and pleasure. Parenthetically, Wordsworth goes to some length to argue that the purpose of providing the reader with the pleasure of poetry in no way constitutes a degradation of the poet's art. To the contrary, such poetry constitutes, in his view, an homage to the dignity of man and a recognition of "the principle of pleasure" that affects all domains of human experience. For Wordsworth, then, poetry emerges from the experience of emotion and involves the poet's expression of his own emotion. He understood the purpose of poetry as the expression of emotion for the purpose of providing pleasure to the reader. Such pleasure was, in his view, no mere indulgence but necessary and natural to humans.

Many others spoke of the central purpose of art as the expression of emotion, including Leo Tolstoy. Though Tolstoy's views are now generally offered as an example of an extreme and untenable form of expressionism, his understanding of the artist's work and purpose was not unlike that held by many others. In his view, the artist, "by means of certain external signs, hands on to others feelings he has lived through, and . . . other people are infected by these feelings, and also experience them."[16] There is, without question, much in Tolstoy's writing that presses his expressionist view well past the boundaries acceptable to even those of an expressionist inclination, particularly as it concerns art and morality; but his insistence that art involves the articulation and communication of human feelings was characteristic of the expressionist view commonly held by his contemporaries.

EXPRESSION AND SIGNIFICATION THEORY IN THE TWENTIETH CENTURY

In the twentieth century, as in the nineteenth, one encounters various emotion-based theories of music and the arts, which increasingly exhibit the influence of formalist thought that has dominated the academic community since the 1920s. As previously noted, when speaking of expression theory, one needs to avoid the suggestion that there exists a single, coherent position concerning the relation of art to emotion. That is to say, expression theory consists of a cluster of ideas rather than a particular and solitary theoretical construct, and there are points of deep disagreement

16. Tolstoy, *What Is Art?*, 50.

among expressionist theorists. Having offered this caution, I want to take as a point of departure a generic sketch, if you will, of the expressionist position that includes its constituent features. According to this theoretical position, the work of the artist involves both a venting and an arousing of emotion, where the composer, poet, painter is: (a) said to experience a particular emotion; (b) while compelled by the experience or memory of that emotion, expresses the "felt" emotion by objectifying and embodying it in a given work; (c) upon encountering the work, the same feeling is aroused in the listener as was experienced initially by the composer and which prompted him or her to express this feeling in the work. Though Tolstoy advocated something quite close to this, few others would now find this particular formulation acceptable. However, with this model in mind, let us proceed to explore several important variants found in philosophical work of the twentieth century.

Among the significant philosophers of the twentieth century to hold an expressionist view are R. G. Collingwood, Curt Ducasse, and George Santayana. In respect to the three-part formulation given above, Collingwood explicitly rejects the idea that arousal of emotion in the percipient has any proper relation to art. Moreover, it is important to note that the process of expression of which Collingwood speaks rejects the idea that the artist, in this context, merely vents or gives utterance to his own feelings. Here, the process of expression involves an artistic process of objectifying *felt* emotion and embodying it. Collingwood was an advocate of the expressive function of art and contended that the task of the artist is to express that which he feels—his own emotions. But the process of expression involved objectifying the emotion, and, in this, the artist differs from one who expresses him or herself by screaming because of pain or laughing in response to a humorous event. In relation to the generic formulation of expression theory previously stated, Collingwood, then, accepts stages *a* and *b* and rejects *c*.

Unlike Collingwood, Ducasse accepts proposition *c*. Like Tolstoy, he suggests that an artwork constitutes a "consciously objective expression of feeling which in contemplation . . . reflects back accurately the feeling which was to be expressed."[17] That is, the work expresses human feeling and evokes that same feeling in the observer. Both writers stress the importance of the fact that what is expressed is no mere description of feeling but something more. Ducasse holds that "the nature of love, fear, hatred, jealousy, or of any

---

17. Ducasse, "Aesthetic Attitude," 358.

other feeling whether named or nameless, is something that no description can impart,"[18] while Collingwood takes the position that description in fact hinders expression inasmuch as it necessarily generalizes, whereas expression individualizes. They do not agree concerning the place of evocation in expression theory, but they share the view that there are qualities and features of human emotive experience that cannot be "described" without considerable loss. The value of art, according to both Collingwood and Ducasse, lies in its capacity to transcend mere description and to embody feeling or emotion in artistic form.

While Collingwood eschews the notion of arousal as a function of art, he does introduce the ancient idea of catharsis: in his view, unexpressed emotion results in emotional oppression which is removed when expressed and permitted to enter into consciousness. The notion of catharsis as a function of art also arises in the work of Santayana. He writes this:

> Thus a man whose physiological complexion involves a more poignant emotion than his ideas can absorb . . . will yearn for new objects that may explain, embody, and focus his dumb feelings; and these objects, if art can produce them, will relieve and glorify those feelings in the act of expressing them. Catharsis is nothing more.[19]

Unlike many philosophers who concerned themselves with aesthetics, Santayana possessed a substantial understanding of music. He understood the uniqueness of music and compared it to mathematics as "very nearly a world by itself."[20] However, given his romantic, emotionalist bias, he was bound to modify his formalist inclinations, and we find evidence of this when he speaks of the relation between music and human experience: "This ethereal art," he says, "may be enticed to earth and married with what is mortal."[21] In his view, it is "the singular privilege of this art . . . to give form to what is naturally inarticulate, and express those depths of human nature which can speak no language current in the world."[22]

Though there are differences among the various models of expression theory, some of which are substantive, one finds here a core concept of art as the expression, the embodiment in artistic form, of feeling. Here lies the central value and purpose of art: its capacity to embody the depths of

18. Ducasse, "Aesthetic Attitude," 370.
19. Santayana, *Life of Reason*, 64.
20. Santayana, *Life of Reason*, 45.
21. Santayana, *Life of Reason*, 53.
22. Santayana, *Life of Reason*, 56.

human emotion, a complexity of human experience understood to lie beyond the reach of ordinary language and scientific discourse.

MUSIC AND EXPRESSION THEORY

Objections to the Application of Expression Theory to Music

Concerning the application of expression theory to music, formalist critics argue that these various formulations are vulnerable on several grounds. Before examining features of particular writers, let us consider some of the basic objections to the application of expressionist theory to music. To begin, one might challenge the assertion that the composer, while compelled by a particular emotion, gives expression to that feeling or emotion by embodying it in his or her work. Clearly, a composer whose intent it is to "express" a quality of sadness, for example, may not necessarily be sad while composing the work; indeed, it would be quite unusual that a composer be subject to a single emotional state throughout what is often a prolonged compositional process.[23] Second, one might ask whether the emotion evoked by the music is the same as that which the work is said to express. Does the listener in fact recover or reconstruct the emotional experience of the composer through the experience of the work? Along this line of inquiry, Monroe Beardsley asks whether our reaction to the observance of sorrow is in fact sorrow or something else—pity, perhaps

Of greater importance is the problem of how one is to decipher the emotive content of a musical work. If the word *express* is to be understood as a relational term, such that x expresses y, then that word holds value only insofar as it is possible to determine the character of y. This, of course, is the vulnerable flank of the theory as it is applied to music. From a formalist perspective, one might say that the generally unsatisfactory responses to the problem of the nature of the relation between the musical work and what it is said to express is fundamentally tied to the fact that it is not reasonable to maintain that x has an objective correlative that is decipherable. For if we seek both evidence and proof of the relation of x to y, then what a work is said to express need be both objectively and generally evident; that is, the work must be understood to express something that is decipherable

---

23. Hindemith, in his attack on the concept of music as an expression of emotion, makes the same point in a more elaborate manner. See Hindemith, *Composer's World*, 35–38.

to the public capable of appreciating the work. It is precisely the failure or perceived failure of expression theorists to sustain the argument of expression as a two-term concept that renders the theory unsatisfactory in much of the philosophical community.

Ways in Which Music Is Said to Stand in Relation to Emotion

Those who support some form of emotion theory argue that there are various ways in which music stands in relation to human emotion and feeling, including imitation, representation, analogy, language, sign, and symbol. Let us look at some of these.

Perhaps the most common of these, if the least philosophically interesting, is the use of imitation in music. Composers use music to imitate many things—birds' song, the sound of rushing water, the lover's sigh. These musical representations or imitations have long had a place in musical composition. But the formalist critic argues that, in the case of the lover's sigh, what is "expressed" is the sound, not human emotion; it is not the languishing of the lover that is represented but the sigh that is imitated. Moreover, the formalist objects that where there is said to be representation of objects of perception, the audience requires a text to provide clues essential to construing the particular reference. Where the work of the composer is more complex and subtle, we often find a shift from mere representation to evocation and intimation, such as in Debussy's *La Mer* or *The Prelude to the Afternoon of a Faun*. To the positivist, the suggestion that music may evoke and intimate is of little threat, as long as it is understood that intimation does not constitute meaning.

To sustain the view that music is capable of meaning and not merely allusion, it has been argued that music in fact constitutes a form of language.[24] The most celebrated example of such an argument is that posed by Deryck Cooke, when he defines a musical vocabulary and explains how it is used to express emotions. In the system he proposes, there exists a series of "close natural correspondences between the emotive effects of certain notes of the scale and their positions in the acoustic hierarchy known as the harmonic series";[25] furthermore, he identifies particular emotional effects of various intervals such as the "heroic" effect of the augmented fourth and

---

24. See the earlier reference to Schopenhauer.
25. Cooke, *Language of Music*, 25.

the "stoic acceptance" or "tragedy" of the minor third.[26] The best explanation Cooke offers in support of his argument for a musical vocabulary is the point he raises concerning the role of convention and musical formulae. This work is widely rejected in the academic community, where the majority opinion is that music, despite the existence of various formulae and conventions that are admittedly cognitively freighted, does not possess a developed vocabulary with fixed meanings; music has no rules of grammar and is incapable of distinguishing between a subject and a comment upon a subject.[27] Music may imitate the darting movement of a fish, but it cannot tell us if it imitates the darting movement of a fish, the scribbling action of an infant, or children playing tag. Music is clearly similar to language in the sense that it has a logical structure, and some of its elements have conventional associations. However, music is not language; it certainly is not a universal language. The peculiar value of music is not found here.

A more promising avenue of inquiry concerning the way in which music may stand in relation to emotion is the view of music as sign and symbol. Here, the artwork is said to signify something beyond the music and musical process; the basis of this signification is the similarity of the formal structure of the music and the structure of a particular psychological process or event. The work's value, then, resides in the fact that this manner of signification is in some way illuminating. Among signification theorists who share the expressionist's assumption that the principal value of art lies in its significant relation to human feeling and emotion are Suzanne Langer, Louis Arnaud Reid, and Paul Hirst.

Unlike many expression theorists, Langer is concerned neither with the expression of the artist's feeling nor the evocation of emotions in the percipient. Her central thesis is that the function of music as art is to symbolize human feeling and to articulate qualities of the emotive life that lie beyond the reach of discursive symbol. Like her, Reid takes the view that art involves signs and symbols, "a kind of 'logos' of its own," and, like Langer, he suggests that the meaning art embodies "cannot be stated in words."[28] Reid differs from Langer on the fundamental question of what it is that art embodies. He argues that it is not emotion itself that is embodied, for, in his view, emotion is too thoroughly subjective to be objectified in

---

26. Cooke, *Language of Music*, 81, 90.

27. For a discussion of proposition theory and the idea of musical compositions as propositions, see Beardsley, *Aesthetics*, 369–78.

28. Reid, *Ways of Knowledge*, 64.

a work. What is expressed or embodied are "values," which he defines as "feelings-about-an-event, a fact, an idea."[29]

Paul Hirst, who addresses the arts more comprehensively, takes a somewhat different tack. He argues that the arts constitute a unique form of knowledge, and art, through its particular elements and materials, has "a significance that parallels the shape and sound of the words and sentences we use in making statements about the physical world."[30] That is, art is like language, but, as non-linguistic symbol, it need not have a specified referent in order to have meaning. The argument that symbol must necessarily have a referent he takes to be a matter of a mistaken understanding of the nature of linguistic symbols. In fact, he dismisses out of hand the idea that a symbol must have an identifiable referent in order to have meaning. Consequently, he has no difficulty in speaking of the arts and their meaning, unlike Langer and Reid, who have resorted to the language of "import" over this particular issue. Hirst sets himself apart from Langer, Reid, and others not only in terms of his position regarding symbol and referent but by proposing the possibility that works of art constitute artistic statements, "stating truths that cannot be communicated in any other way."[31]

Of the three, it is arguably Langer's work that has had the greatest influence and been the most frequently cited in support of the idea that music, as symbol, articulates that which is beyond the capacity of language to express. It is her view that music as "presentational" symbol articulates or gives form to emotional experience, something that she believes lies beyond the capacity of "discursive" symbol.[32] This it does on the strength of the logical similarity between the structure of the symbol and the structure of emotional experience. Music, then, is expressive of human feelings and holds expressive import, if not meaning. As noted, Langer intentionally avoids the term *meaning* because of the problem of the absence of a named, identifiable referent. This value, then, is designated as import rather than meaning.

The fact that Langer's signification theory is so favorably received in educational circles in Britain and North America is not difficult to appreciate. It is a subtle and complex argument that lends to music and to music

---

29. Reid, *Ways of Knowledge*, 69.
30. Hirst, *Knowledge and the Curriculum*, 152.
31. Hirst, *Knowledge and the Curriculum*, 153.
32. Langer offers a summary of her position concerning music as symbolic form in *Feeling and Form*, 31–32.

education a significance beyond the specifically musical. As Munroe Beardsley points out with respect to signification theory in general, "it offers an interesting possibility, that of construing music as in some sense a special 'language of the emotions,' a discourse about the tensions and torments of the mind, of a different order from ordinary verbal discourse."[33]

Critics of symbol theory and its application to music argue that it is difficult to appreciate why that which Langer ascribes as unconsummated symbol ought to be seen as *symbolizing* anything. Specifically, what does it mean to say that music articulates the forms of feeling? Can the idea of presentational symbol be distinguished from discursive symbol[34]—a theory Langer developed based upon Wittgenstein's picture theory presented in his *Tractatus Logico-Philosophicus*? Can a symbol be a symbol and have no fixed or named referent? And why should the value of music be sought in that which is external to the music, whether it is emotion or anything else?

At first glance, the idea of music as an iconic sign of the emotive life seems to be plausible, insofar as it relates to the kinetic properties of music, where the potential for metaphorical applications is considerable. It is clearly possible to conceive of music as strident, angular, or lilting, on the basis of its (metaphorical) qualities of movement. The presence of such qualities in a musical work is verifiable by examination of the work's musical construct; indeed, it is the application of formal analysis that not only justifies but gives meaning to aesthetic judgments such as "The music is of a lilting character," or "This march is stirring."[35] However, these characterizations seem to be useful only insofar as they have a basis in musical fact and as the listener or performer is able to understand and interpret the musical work—its materials and particular construct—in this way. This, it seems, is still a very long way from successfully demonstrating that music is capable of communicating particular and highly individualized emotive meaning or import that words cannot accommodate. Yet this is precisely the argument of Langer, Reid, and Hirst, among others.

In the final analysis, this is the principal objection of the formalist to signification and expression theories alike: each of these theories points away from the music to that which it is said to express or signify. To refer again to Beardsley, "When descriptions are put into the form of descriptions, they back up their claims by the music itself, and they lead attention

---

33. Beardsley, *Aesthetics*, 337.
34. Beardsley, *Aesthetics*, 337.
35. See Hungerland, "Once Again."

to the music. When they are put in the form of statements about signification, they lead away from the music, very often either into biographical intentionalism disguised as musicological expertness or affective free-associationism disguised as semiotical profundity."[36]

The Inclination to Interrelate Domains of Human Experience

Despite the problems that expression theory and signification theories raise, and notwithstanding the articulate and forceful criticism directed toward them (which has been only briefly summarized here), the fact remains that we are inclined to seek ways to construct meaning of human experience, and, accordingly, we are inclined to relate one thing to another, to continually attempt to construct a whole, an interpretive framework that enables us to make sense of our world and our experience. Accordingly, we make connections, transferences, and associations between the arts and other experience in ways that are admittedly vague and equivocal. With respect to music, the common inclination is to perceive music in metaphorical terms, to see and hear it as insinuation and illusion, to ascribe to it significance beyond the purely musical, despite reasoned objections. The matter of constructing meaning of musical experience we shall consider at greater length in our treatment of the role of metaphor in musical experience in a subsequent chapter.

NOTES FOR THE CHURCH

The Expression of Human Emotion through Worship, Praise, and Prayer

In the course of our personal spiritual journey, each of us seeks to know God and be known by him. This knowing we pursue encompasses both cognitive perception and a mode of knowledge that is primarily experiential. The first is a rational process undergirded by concepts of God's qualities and character—his omniscience, omnipresence, righteousness, goodness, faithfulness, and nature as a loving, merciful, and just God. The second involves knowing through encounter, through experience. With respect to the latter, one of the principal ways we experience God is through the act

---

36. Beardsley, *Aesthetics*, 338.

of giving praise, our expression of joy and thankfulness to God. Indeed, the Scriptures enjoin us to be a people who give unstintingly of their praise, for such praise constitutes the sacrifice of a jubilant and thankful heart, which both honors and glorifies God and brings us into a place of communion with him.

Such praise is the appropriate and dutiful response of grateful hearts, but it is also critical to attaining an increased knowledge of and intimacy with the divine Creator whose desire it is to be known.[37] Consequently, the Scriptures abound with texts that underscore the imperative that the people of God are to be a people of praise and thanksgiving. We are exhorted to praise God with our voices and with instruments. Psalm 98 says, "Make a joyful noise to the Lord, all the earth; break forth into joyous song and sing praises. Sing praises to the Lord with the lyre, with the lyre and the sound of melody. With trumpets and the sound of the horn make a joyful noise before the King, the Lord." This exhortation resounds throughout the Old Testament Scriptures. "Be glad in the Lord and rejoice, O righteous, and shout for joy, all you upright in heart" (Ps 32:11). In Deuteronomy 16:11, we read, "Rejoice before the Lord your God—you and your sons and your daughters, your male and female slaves, the Levites resident in your towns, as well as the strangers, the orphans, and the widows who are among you— at the place that the Lord your God will choose as a dwelling for his name." In Zephaniah 3:14, the prophet's exhortation takes this form: "Sing aloud, O daughter Zion; shout, O Israel! Rejoice and exult with all your heart, O daughter Jerusalem!" In Zechariah 9:9, we encounter the magnificent prophetic text that begins with the exhortation to rejoice: "Rejoice greatly, O daughter Zion! Shout aloud, O daughter Jerusalem! Lo, your king comes to you; triumphant and victorious is he, humble and riding on a donkey, on a colt, the foal of a donkey." In First Samuel 2:1, Hannah speaks of giving voice to the abundant and overflowing emotions of the heart when she says, "My heart exults in the Lord; my strength is exalted in my God. My mouth derides my enemies, because I rejoice in my victory."

The New Testament is also replete with texts that encourage the people to rejoice in God their Savior. Saint Paul in his Letter to the Philippians enjoins the church to rejoice in the Lord, to give voice and expression to their joy in God and their life in Christ. "Rejoice in the Lord always; again I

---

37. See Jer 31:33: "But this is the covenant that I will make with the house of Israel after those days, says the Lord: I will put my law within them, and I will write it on their hearts; and I will be their God, and they shall be my people."

will say, Rejoice" (Phil 4:4). One encounters other such exhortations in the writings of Saint Paul, including texts found in Romans, Thessalonians, and Corinthians. Additionally, in the Epistle of Saint Peter (1 Pet 1:8), we find the exquisite statement about loving the One we have not seen but the One in whom we believe: "Although you have not seen him, you love him; and even though you do not see him now, you believe in him and rejoice with an indescribable and glorious joy." How rich and profound is the emotion that prompts this poetic utterance.

In fact, our communication with God through praise and prayer encompasses the full range of human emotion, just as our communication with God has many purposes. When we sing or pray, either in the context of collective worship or private prayer, we may seek to praise God, or we may focus on affirming our existence as a spiritual community and proclaim our commitment to various theological beliefs; we may petition God with respect to our concerns and needs, or we may intercede on behalf of others. Prayers of petition and intercession occupy a large place in our life of prayer and communion with God; and given that these prayers emerge from our needs and desires as well as the needs of others, they are frequently emotively freighted. I pray for an improvement in my mother's eyesight, for the mental health of a struggling friend, for the pressures experienced by family and friends as a consequence of a financial downturn. I pray for wisdom to better engage with a friend or spouse with whom I am experiencing conflict or with a child whose behavior I find confounding. In all these situations, my response to life's realities and my communication with God concerning them is deeply enmeshed with my emotional response to the world I inhabit—my experience of anxiety, fear, sorrow, frustration, worry, guilt, yearning, dismay, and possibly rage. Each of these emotions is part of the fabric of our human existence and lies at the very heart of our communication with God.

Of course, prayer is not only words, nor is it only a matter of telling God about ourselves. As Edward Farrell puts it, "Prayer is a waiting. It is hunger, it is love. Prayer is a relatedness, and prayer is stillness." As Farrell submits, "Prayer, rightly understood, is an expression of the deepest levels of our being. Prayer for the Christian is always a response to the living Christ, to the living Person."[38] In the Christian life, the people of God give expression to that innermost part of themselves in ways both articulate and

---

38. Farrell, *Beams of Prayer*, 18.

inarticulate, even the groanings of the spirit by which the Spirit of God prays for us and with us.

The Place of the Arts in Christian Prayer and Praise

As we consider the various means by which we communicate with God and give expression to "the deepest levels of our being," the question arises concerning the place of art and the beautiful in this aspect of the believer's life and spiritual experience; and, as we pursue the matter, we come to the conclusion that, in some contexts, art and the beautiful play a profound part in the praise, worship, and prayer of the church, while, in others, the arts may be of little consequence whatsoever. As noted, part of what we do as we worship God is give expression to our feelings before the Lord. So let us begin then with the idea of self-expression in the context of praise and prayer and examine the place of the arts in such activity.

As noted in the earlier part of this chapter, significance has been ascribed to the arts—whether poetry, literature, music, painting, or other forms of art—for many reasons, but primary among them is their powerful connection with human emotion. The particular nature of this relationship has been variously understood as a means of venting of emotion through performance and composition (catharsis), as the representation of emotion through imitation, or as the symbolizing or signifying of emotion. I will not repeat here these matters already treated in this chapter. However, there is another function previously discussed which is of particular relevance to worship in the contemporary church and which needs further elaboration, namely, the idea that music and the spoken word, as well as others of the arts, may function or may be understood to function as a means of self-expression.

It is important to note that there is unquestionably much great art in the domains of music, poetry, and iconography, among others, that contributes to the diverse praise and worship that occurs in the life of the church. That said, it is imperative to note that self-expression, that is, the expression of personal feeling, does not typically involve the objectification of human feeling and the embodiment of this feeling in artistic form. Rather, the chief object in the context of worship is the expression of personal emotion and, possibly, the communication of ideas. This is to say that where we seek principally to communicate with God and to give expression to our feelings, thoughts, and desires, we are not typically preoccupied with producing in our worship a work or object that objectifies our feelings. We are not principally concerning with art-making.

Concerning the question of the relevance of self-expression to art, Suzanne Langer argues that the artwork is of consequence precisely because of its particular character and its capacity to lead us beyond ourselves. What we discover in art is that which it abstracts for perception. It is this "objectivity and potency of the commanding form that commands our attention."[39] According to this view, preoccupation with self-expression shares little ground with art-making. And yet, when one speaks of music in worship and the relevance of self-expression in acts of prayer and praise, there are certainly moments when a particular quality of the music, even as what might be termed "art" music, coincides with a worshiper's personal feeling. In such a situation, the performance of a musical offering in the context of singing or listening to the music of an instrument, voice, or choir or the reading of a text may well involve and evoke a personal expression of emotion, a venting of emotion, if you will. Yet, the objection of Langer and others to self-expression in terms of its relation to art is, I suspect, valid.

In general, the making of art music and art more broadly understood entails a process that focuses on the technical, structural, and interpretative demands of the work, a process that provides little allowance for the venting of personal emotion. The artistic process is largely self-contained in the sense that it necessitates building and exploring an artistic world, an expressive world, in terms of its own materials, compositional devices, and conventions. So, where an organist performs a Bach partita as part of a service, as an organist, she or he concentrates principally on the demands of the score, its technical and expressive elements. The same is true of the choir performing a sung portion of the Mass, for example. While there may be an element of this complex process that involves the expression of personal emotion, for the most part, the responsibility of the ensemble is to attend to the musical requirements and demands of the composition and the conductor in the realization of the score. This is not to deny that art-making may at times involve expression of personal feeling; it is, however, to say that the process of self-expression rarely involves art-making.

---

39. Langer, *Feeling and Form*, 131.

Beyond Self-Expression

While the making or performing of art may be said to stand in tension with the process of self-expression, there is much to human expression that extends beyond self-expression. The arts understood as broadly including but not limited to music, poetry, literature, the drama of the liturgy, architecture, sculpture in wood and stone, painting, and tapestry have long functioned as servants in the life and work of the church. The arts have illuminated and embodied the theology of the church in the church's painting, sculpture, and stained glass; the spiritual life of the church has been vivified through the church's music, both sung and played; the needs and desires of the hearts and minds of the people of God have been articulated with subtlety and depth through the magnificent prayers of the ancient liturgy of the church, whether in Latin or in the vernacular, and in the spiritual poetry of many from Milton, St. John of the Cross, John Donne, and George Herbert, to William Blake, Gerard Manley Hopkins, C. S. Lewis, and W. H. Auden, along with more recent poets such as Margaret Avison and Malcolm Guite. Over the centuries, the arts have provided a magnificent body of expressive materials in a variety of media and genres that give voice to the deepest and most complex of human emotions and have enabled the faithful to give expression to emotions both named and unnamed. Assuredly, the great Christian art of the church has been vital to the spiritual practice of the church. For not only does it explore and give voice to the emotions of the heart, but, at times, these works have led us into the very presence of God. As Pope Benedict put it, we have so often experienced the great art of the church as epiphany: we have encountered God in the midst of the beauty of these magnificent works.

Philosophers and art theorists throughout the ages were correct in making a foundational connection between the arts and human emotion. And, if Suzanne Langer is correct, the arts have the capacity to enable us to experience and give expression to a richer array of emotional content than we might otherwise encounter. This broadening of our emotional world is part of the human striving to become more of what God has made possible for us as individuals and as the church.

The Rejection of High Art in Worship and Praise

Whatever the value of the great art of the church, the fact remains that the universal church is a highly diverse and complex theological and social reality, and much of the contemporary church, wherever it is situated, no longer finds the great art traditions of the past conducive to spiritual life and practice. The great musical masses and chant repertoire of the church, for example, are now irrelevant to many, and the poetical texts and dramatic elements of the liturgy are oftentimes perceived as obstacles to authentic worship. Throughout much of the church, the high art forms of organ music and choral literature have given way to colloquial musics that are regarded as music of the people, and this is true of a cross section of the arts throughout the life and practice of the church, both Catholic and Protestant. What was once regarded as high art is now commonly replaced by more colloquial, accessible, and utilitarian works of craft that, in a very different manner, give expression to the emotional and theological needs and interests of the church.

In the midst of the cultural turmoil and frequent dissension concerning the nature of the beautiful, and the radical increase in the variety and genres of music and other art forms that are now found in the service of the church, there continues for many a commitment to giving to God the best of our talents, irrespective of the compositional style and genre. There remains a commitment to artistry.

Artistry in Worship and Praise

The matter of artistry in the preparation and performance of worship and praise is relevant whatever mode of music and liturgical form is utilized in the life of the church. In the Taizé community, for example, the music is comprised of beautiful but simple melodies and harmonic language combined with short poetic texts that are offered as prayer. The simplicity of the music and text make it possible for the communicant to sing, to praise and worship, and to listen for the prompting and voice of God. There is a musical ease and beauty that contributes to a sense of timelessness that encourages the believer to lose him or herself in the presence of God. And yet, artistry remains important in this context. In speaking of artistry, I refer to all that one intends in speaking of craftmanship and workmanship, of commitment and attention to the technical demands of the work, with all the attentiveness and skill of which one is capable. The work of genuine craft admits no disinterest or laziness. The instrumental voices are prepared, and, where a liturgical leader is available, his or her part is to press for that which is artistically and expressively refined. This gift of our sung prayers is a gift of our best. The manner of our music-making and craft matters. These are gifts of our talents and labor offered to God, whether as amateurs or persons of craft possessing a cultivated skill. In other contexts, the church utilizes choruses and gospel hymns as musical materials that approximate the vernacular as a means of communicating intense personal feelings directed toward God. Here, too, the matter of artistry is crucial. Church musicians, both instrumentalists and church choirs, meet regularly for rehearsal in order to give the best of their talents to God. This is a self-giving that promotes artful action undertaken as an act of praise.

The forms and content of the arts are many, but we are able to agree that they ought to be performed with a disciplined and attentive preparation to the expressive demands of the particular work, irrespective of the medium or genre. This we do to the glory of God.

4

Formalism Revisited and Revised

INTRODUCTION

THIS CHAPTER OFFERS A REVIEW of the central tenets of formalist theory and that theory's primary thesis that the central value of the artwork lies in its properties. This view of art focuses on what and how the work is rather than what it does or means and asserts that authentic and mature engagement with a work necessarily involves a measure of knowledge of the work and its compositional features. That is, it assumes a critical relationship between comprehension and apprehension in the matter of one's experience of works of art. Pivotal to this chapter, then, is the question "What does it mean to know a work?" and an exploration of the role of knowledge of form—the form of the work—in aesthetic experience. This discussion leads to a way of approaching works of art that is influenced by a formalist perspective, while embracing the significance of context and the legitimate place of emotion and subjective response in aesthetic activity. Despite a formalist bias, there is no diminishment here of the significance of a percipient's emotive response to artworks, for it is our belief that a rich artistic/aesthetic experience is characterized by an inter-illumination of the two domains, where cognition informs feeling and feeling cognition.

What is proposed is not merely the detached knowing of an object that is consciously distanced from the listener but an interaction between the knower and the known—a process that Treitler speaks of as being "engulfed in and surrounded by the known"[1]—an image that suggests an

---

1. Treitler, *Music and Historical Imagination*, 10.

intimacy between the I and the musical or artistic Thou, where the other is not merely a passing acquaintance but the *known*. The musical or aesthetic experience of any artwork, irrespective of the medium or genre—which is characterized here as mature and authentic—embraces the pleasure of the senses and the beauty of reason. The central thesis of this argument, then, is that not just any passion or emotive response, however intense, properly characterizes the relation between listener and an artistic work, but only that borne of a genuine interaction and experience of the work as that which is known.

There are, of course, countless stages or states of knowing a poem, painting, or musical composition, ranging from an initial hearing, reading, or exposure to an intimacy with the work and a deep understanding of its compositional and expressive features. But we may make a beginning by speaking of coming to a work in a way that is progressive and cumulative—a process that may involve a lifetime. In this way, the work unfolds as the percipient is increasingly able to grasp the significance of the artistic concept and design and able to receive consciously and unconsciously the formal and sensual aspects of the work, which are, in fact, inseparable. The process involves repeated encounters; in the case of a musical work, a repeated hearing or performing of the work and a discovery of the facts of the musical event—pitches, rhythms, timbres, tempi, melodies, motifs—and the relations of such events within the work. Second, the work comes to be understood as one among others of its kind; that is, the work is progressively received in a compositional context. Third, the discerning of the work's authentic voice requires an understanding of the conventions that contribute to the compositional style that characterizes the work and that has influenced the compositional process and product. Last in this particular list is the matter of recognizing the work as it was heard when first performed, as it was perceived and received at the time of the work's composition. In the last few decades, performers, scholars, and teachers have become increasingly interested in reclaiming and understanding the great literature of the past in terms of its historical voice and character. This is true also for the world of theater.

The task of recovering and receiving a work in its fullness is a formidable business and one for which most twentieth-century listeners have little patience. Yet whether or not we have the taste for it, the fact remains that the experience of the work is transformed by what is known of the work and the conditions that frame it. As Treitler observes, this knowledge of the work is not for the purpose of "explaining" it in terms of its "conventions and antecedents," but as a means of embracing the work and grasping the "values and schemata" that conditioned the creation of the work. The goal of musical analysis, he says, is "the conditioning of the listener for perceptive hearing."[2] This is the principal contribution of formalist theory to musical experience. It asserts the significance of knowledge as a ground for perceptive hearing, which provides the critical tools necessary to embrace the work in terms of its own "values and schemata." By extension, the same may be said for any of the arts, for they all possess their own distinctive materials, compositional devices, strategies, and values.

FORMALIST THEORY IN MUSIC, ART, AND LITERATURE

Since the time of the ancient Greeks, philosophers have concerned themselves with questions concerning the nature of beauty and its particular value, speculation which has given rise to numerous theories of art, including art as representation and imitation; art as the beautiful and a mode of the good; art as expression, language, communication, and symbol; and art as form. Each of these theories or schools of thought is, in fact, marked by variants that caution against any presumption of homogeneity. The latter category, art as form, is separated from all the rest on account of its rejection of the fundamental proposition that the value of art rests on the capacity to express, symbolize, or otherwise communicate emotional states or feelings—or anything else, for that matter. As previously noted, the positive formalist thesis is that the value of art lies in its manner of being, in its form and structure, and that art is valuable for its own sake. That is, its value lies in what it is and not what it does.

Concerning music, Eduard Hanslick argued both this positive and negative thesis. The latter, in which he articulates his opposition to the notion that feeling is the content of music, occupies the first two chapters of his famous treatise *On the Musically Beautiful* (1854). I quote from the text at length, for though it was written a century and a half ago, it remains as one of the most eloquent statements of the formalist view:

> There has been considerable agreement that the whole gamut of human feelings is the content of music, because feelings were considered to be the opposite of conceptual definiteness, hence they are a proper criterion for the distinction between music on the

[2]. Treitler, *Music and Historical Imagination*, 71–72.

> one hand and the visual and literary arts on the other. In this view, tones and their elaborate combination would be nothing more than raw material, the medium of expression, by means of which the composer represents love, courage, piety, rapture. These feelings, in their rich variety, would be the Idea which has attired itself in the earthly body of physical sound in order that it may walk on earth here below as a musical artwork. That which in a lovely melody or an ingenious harmony delight and lifts us up would be not these in themselves but what they signify: the whisperings of amorousness, the violence of conflict.
>
> In order to get on firm ground, we must first relentlessly get rid of such tired cliches.... The representation of a specific feeling or emotional state is not at all among the characteristic powers of music.[3]

With respect to the idea of content, Hanslick contends that music is constituted of "tonal sequences, tonal forms"; "these," he argues, "have no other content than themselves."[4] This, he suggests, separates music from the literary and visual arts, which clearly have a capacity to represent thoughts, feelings, and events.

The preceding excerpt hints at the substance of the positive thesis when he implies that the "lovely melody or an ingenious harmony" are a delight to the listener "in themselves." Though at pains to confront and discredit the negative premise, Hanslick speaks eloquently to the question of the central value of music when he asks, "What kind of beauty is the beauty of a musical composition?" His answer: "It is a specifically musical kind of beauty ... that consists simply and solely of tones and their artistic combination."[5] The value of music is its beauty, and its beauty is found in its form.

A primary consequence of the negative premise is the elimination of most of the connections commonly made between art and human experience—connections that form the basis of the value of art, in the minds of many. This separation of art and ordinary life is a particularly salient feature of the formalist theory of Clive Bell, in which philosophy of art was strongly linked to Bell's interest and expertise in the visual arts. In a volume entitled *Art* (1914), Bell argues that the representative element of a work is irrelevant to the work as a work of art. What is important, he suggests,

---

3. Hanslick, *On the Musically Beautiful*, 8–9.
4. Hanslick, *On the Musically Beautiful*, 78.
5. Hanslick, *On the Musically Beautiful*, 28.

is its "significant form": "lines and colors combined in a particular way, certain forms and relations of forms" constitute this significant form.[6] Bell goes so far as to say that "to appreciate a work of art we need bring with us nothing from life, no knowledge of its ideas and affairs, no familiarity with its emotions."[7] According to this view, art owes little to human experience, and the experience of art stands entirely separate from other experience. Art tells us nothing of life, of truth; it tells us nothing of ourselves, our culture or history. At least, as art, it has no value in these terms. The emotions that it stirs are aesthetic emotions and not the ordinary emotions of life. The significance of a work is, therefore, "unrelated to the significance of life."[8] Roger Fry, a contemporary of Bell, also emphasized the separation of art and life. The creative vision, the highest order of perception and contemplation of the visual field, demands, he says, "the most complete detachment from any of the meanings and implications of appearances." When viewed in this manner, even the most profound subject "becomes of no more significance than any casual piece of matter."[9]

In literary theory, the formalists were also strongly inclined to separate the significance of art from values associated with that considered extrinsic to literature. Formalist literary scholar Grigorij Vinokur, referring to the work of the Russian formalists—Boris Eichenbaum, Viktor Shklovsky, Roman Jakobson, and Yuri Tynyanov, among others—informs us of their interest in *"literature itself,* and not anything else."[10] Their work, generated in Moscow and St. Petersburg in the early decades of the twentieth century, focused on the structure of literary works, discounting altogether any scholarly consideration of linkages between the literary work and biographical information concerning the author or other social or historical factors external to the work.

Terence Hawkes's assessment of the formalist view is that it perceived literature as "isolatable, separable from what goes on beyond it, and thus, like language itself, perceivable as a structure ... whole, capable of transformation, self-regulating, autonomous and internally coherent."[11] This characterization of formalist theory applied to literature is equally applicable

6. Bell, *Art*, 8.
7. Bell, *Art*, 25.
8. Bell, *Art*, 26–27.
9. Fry, *Vision and Design*, 33–34.
10. Grigorij Vinokur, as cited in Steiner, *Russian Formalism*, 245; emphasis in original.
11. Hawkes, *Structuralism and Semiotics*, 71.

to the formalist argument of Hanslick and Bell that was dominant in the musical academy in Western countries for much of the twentieth century.

While a substantial argument can be made that formalist theory, at least to the extent that Hawkes's characterization is legitimate, is fundamentally reductionist, we leave this critique aside for the moment to focus on what is accepted as fundamental to a formalist view and of importance in the first order to the argument presented here—specifically, the view that art places demands on its audience. It is the task of the reader, listener, or observer, according to the formalist view, to come to grips with the work's structure—its internal relations and patterns of coherence. As readers, listeners, observers who would be marked as those of a discerning ear and eye, we accept the importance of coming to a fuller and more genuine appreciation of artworks by seeking a thorough knowledge of those works that appeal to us, that speak to us, and recognize that critical and informed analysis is essential to such experience, though it may not be consciously exercised in each encounter with a work. This is simply to affirm the maxim that knowledge of the work enriches, clarifies, and intensifies our perception of the work and our experience of it.

THE DISCERNING EAR AND EYE

With respect to artistic and aesthetic activity, it is important to appreciate the significant distinction between looking and seeing, and between listening and hearing. The ability to see and hear is predicated, to some considerable extent, upon the capacity to perceive the significant order of a work, to recognize the function of its various elements in the construct as a whole, and to perceive its internal relations and compositional device. In the routine experience of our lives, much of what we perceive is received and processed in a manner that is cognitively passive or precritical. What we seek in relation to our engagement with works of art, at least some of the time and in domains in which we have a measure of technical competence, is an experience of the work that is intense and critically active: an experience marked by a process of perception and judgment that involves making "delicate discriminations and discerning subtle relationships," as Goodman suggests.[12]

The value or benefit that accrues to those with the capacity for discrimination and discernment rests on our experience that art offers an

---

12. Goodman, *Problems and Projects*, 103. Goodman offers a vigorous defence of the active and analytical disposition of the aesthetic attitude.

Formalism Revisited and Revised

intensification of ordinary experience or, more properly, that authentic experience of art enables us to transcend the ordinary; and that the nature of such engagement with the work involves a process of clarifying and interpreting the artistic world under consideration, its compositional principles and patterns, much of which is not immediately evident to the uninitiated. To experience the riches of the worlds of literature, dance, music, and sculpture, we participate in them, and, increasingly, this participation is marked by a high order of thinking and feeling. The process of making "delicate discriminations and discerning subtle relationships" (to borrow Goodman's phrase) necessitates the operation of a critical capacity, which enables one to see rather than merely to look and to hear what is there to be heard.

What follows are several examples that illustrate the significance of the educative and analytical process in aesthetic experience. Here, we examine how knowledge of the work and the artistic world of which it is part transforms our perception of the work and our understanding of its artistic value. I have chosen three examples: an eighteenth-century European opera, a painting from the same period, and a tenth-century Balinese architectural structure. Though the examples may be remote, these magnificent artworks serve well the purposes of the argument.

The first example is a Baroque opera, *Giulio Cesare*, composed by Handel, with a libretto by Nicola Francesco Haym. The opera, first performed in London in 1724, is scored for string orchestra, four horns, two oboes, flutes, trombone, bassoon, theorbo, harp, and cembalo. Though splendidly orchestrated for a few extravagant scenes, much of the opera is, in fact, scored as a chamber work for strings, or strings and a wind instrument. The grand moments include both the opening and closing choruses and the remarkable sinfonia and introduction to the second act that utilizes two orchestras, one in the pit and the other on the stage, and has Cleopatra depicted as Virtue on Mount Parnassus, surrounded by the nine Muses.

The opera takes as its plot Caesar's travel to Egypt, following Pompey, his defeated rival. In Alexandria, he encounters Cleopatra and Tolomeo, her brother and co-regent. The drama centers on Caesar's infatuation with Cleopatra; his conflict with Tolomeo, who attempts to murder him; and the fate of Cornelia, the widow of the slain Pompey, and her young adult stepson, Sesto. The opera is visually striking, exploiting its exotic location, the heroic character of Caesar, and both the beauty and seductiveness of Cleopatra, the young Egyptian queen.

In musical terms, *opera seria*, as this musical and theatrical genre came to be known, is essentially a high-voice art form, which placed a premium on the vocal art of the castrato, a voice type extraordinarily popular in eighteenth-century Europe. These male singers, the best of whom were vocally powerful and technically highly skilled, possessed a female vocal range—either soprano, mezzo-soprano, or contralto—with a unique vocal timbre. The role of Caesar was written for such a voice and sung by Senesino, a celebrated contralto castrato. The role of Cleopatra was undertaken by the renowned soprano Francesca Cuzzoni. For each of the two principals, Handel composed eight arias that abound with exquisite melodic and harmonic material. Also noteworthy is the duet of Cornelia and Sesto that concludes the first act. Here, Handel demonstrates extraordinary lyrical skill in an exquisite portrayal of the pathos that attends the bereaved and importuned Cornelia and her stepson. The duet is all the more remarkable given that it is written for comparatively minor characters.

Despite its striking visual and musical qualities, this work poses genuine obstacles to the modern audience, particularly those uninitiated in the conventions of Baroque opera. First, the heroic role of Caesar sung by a female voice type is startling to many accustomed to the nineteenth-century operatic model in which the heroic male role would typically be cast as a tenor or baritone. Though the convention was commonplace in the eighteenth century, it is certainly strange to the modern audience accustomed to romantic opera. The love duet between Cleopatra and Caesar that precedes the closing chorus, a duet of a soprano and a contralto voice, is most certainly complicated for much of the modern audience whose frame of reference is the conventions of romantic opera.

Second, the dramaturgy of Baroque opera poses a substantial obstacle to the expectations of modern audiences. For example, in *opera seria*, the entrances and exits of characters were strictly governed by convention, such that at the conclusion of an aria, the singer was bound to leave the stage. In accordance with this exit convention, Sesto, having proclaimed his intent to revenge his father's murder, leaves the stage. The result of this convention was a preponderance of threatened, as opposed to consummated, action. Moreover, the staging was typically blocked in such a way that there was little or no movement during the arias. Again, the conventions of the period result in a lack of dramatic realism. This was not problematic for a Baroque audience, but the modern audience, notwithstanding the dramatic oddities of nineteenth-century opera, anticipates a more lifelike engagement of actors on stage.

These factors—the predominance of high voice types, including the heroic male roles, combined with the absence of a dramatic realism due to the staging conventions of the period—constitute substantial challenges to modern sensibilities. For many, particularly the uninitiated, it is difficult to see and hear Baroque opera for what it is and what it is intended to be, rather than what it is not.

Second, let us consider *The Intervention of the Sabine Women*, a painting by Jacques-Louis David (1799). The artist depicts two warring parties, one on the left and the other on the right of the canvas. Bows are drawn and spears ready; and at the warriors' feet lie some who have already perished in the battle. Separating the two warring factions are a group of women, several of whom hold children in their arms. Among them stands a woman who faces a group of poised archers, holding above her head an infant child. How the women and children came into the middle of the battle is, of course, not clear from the painting alone. However, the title of the painting refers to a legendary battle between two peoples. Plutarch's record of this encounter begins with the abduction and rape of the Sabine women by the Romans. As Plutarch relates the story, several years had passed before the Sabine men returned to liberate the women and exact revenge. By this time, the Sabine women had established relationships with the Roman men as husbands and fathers of their children. Plutarch informs us that "the daughters of the Sabines came running, in great confusion, some on this side, some on that, with miserable cries and lamentations, like creatures possessed, in the midst of the army and among the dead bodies, to come at their husbands and their fathers, some with their young babies in their arms." In the midst of the battle, they cried out, "Do not rob us of our children and husbands. Make us not, we entreat you, twice captives."[13] Clearly, the reference to Sabine women in the title of the painting is important to the experience of the work, for knowledge of this particular historical event lends a new understanding to the psychological state of the women depicted in the painting. The force of the narrative rests on recognition of the fact that the encounter depicted follows the women's abduction and rape. To be ignorant of this is to be confounded by the partial narrative provided in the painting and to remain incapable of making an informed judgment concerning the work. However, for those familiar with the story,

13. Plutarch, *Plutarch's Lives*, 24.

this pictorial representation of the Sabine women recalls a poignant legend that is highly evocative and part of the fabric of Western culture.

The argument I propose is that the painting does not have an independent existence, nor should it be isolated in our experience. The artist has offered a particular perspective on the narrative or part of the narrative that is of artistic consequence and interpretive force, and thereby contributed to the fabric of the narrative. But the work is not merely an objective description of an event; neither is it merely a matter of form and color, with incidental reference to a legendary tale. In our viewing and contemplation of the work, the narrative may at times be eclipsed by the form, and the form at times eclipsed by the narrative. The fullness of the work is experienced, as Panofsky suggests, as a unity of form, idea, and content.[14]

The relevance of the subject matter to one's experience of the work is, or so it seems to me, tied to the more fundamental matter of whether the narrative content is important to the painting. If the narrative content is important to the work, then it is also important to our experience of the work—or, at least, it ought to be. Moreover, the process of participating fully in the work will then necessitate not only a perception of the work's formal properties but appreciation of the narrative content of the painting and, in this particular case, a knowledge of the broader narrative to which the work alludes.

This suggestion is, of course, contrary to the views of formalists such as Fry and Bell who held that the story depicted in a painting, or what is here referred to as its narrative content, is unimportant to the artistic value of the work and that the value of the work lies entirely in its form and color. This position has been held by many formalists, but I believe it constitutes an unnecessarily narrow approach to representative painting and, by implication, to the role of signification and allusion in artworks in general. Kenneth Clark places this conservative formalistic view in a broader historical perspective when he suggests that "Giotto, Giovanni Bellini, Titian, Michelangelo, Poussin, or Rembrandt would have thought it incredible that so absurd a doctrine could have gained currency."[15]

It is, I suggest, the privilege of painting and literature to address the human condition in a manner that music cannot: both art and literature are able to record and comment upon human perception, thought, and action. In the case of representative painting, the artist's commentary is, of course,

---

14. Panofsky, *Meaning in Visual Arts*, 16.
15. See Kenneth Clark's introduction in Hall, *Dictionary of Subjects*, vii.

inferred. The work cannot "speak" of death or sorrow but can demonstrate or represent these human feelings through visual images of the agony of the dying and the bereaved. The stories of Orpheus and Eurydice, the death of Socrates, the sacrifice of Isaac resonate throughout the centuries and continue to enlarge our experience of what it is to be human in the present. This is the work of myth and symbol, and it does not cease to inform our experience when it occurs in the form of pictorial narrative. The challenge that many observers encounter is their inability to interpret the significance of works that incorporate literary or historical reference or religious or secular symbol; for these observers, the task of cultivating a knowledge of the historical and cultural context pertinent to the work is an essential part of coming to know the work. This difficulty is, of course, even more pronounced in cross-cultural contexts where the percipient is ignorant of the symbolic significance of the work and the cultural values that function as a basis for ascribing value and meaning to the work.

Third, let us consider two examples of Balinese religious architecture: the Tirta Empul temple in Bali (926 AD), a temple dedicated to Vishnu, the Hindu god of water; and the Palasari Catholic Church (circa 1956), formally known as the Church of the Sacred Heart Parish of Jesus, located in the Palasari hamlet in western Bali. Specifically, we consider the presence and significance of the Bhoma in Balinese Hindu temple architecture and its absence in the architecture of the Palasari Catholic Church. The Balinese and their Javanese cousins have developed over the centuries a highly refined practice of carving, both in wood and stone. Evidence of this remarkable artistic practice is found in the thousands of temples, ancient and modern, found throughout Bali and the island of Java. In Balinese Hindu architecture, the temple is an open-air construct with walled compounds, which is characteristically divided into three parts: the outer sanctum, or *nistaning mandala*; the middle sanctum, or *madya mandala*; and the inner sanctum, the holiest part of the temple, which is called the *utamaning mandala*.[16] There are typically two gates to be found in a Balinesian temple compound,[17] the first of which is the gate to the outer sanctum or the initial entrance to the temple grounds. This is the split gate, or *candi bentar*, an unroofed, symmetrical gateway that creates a passage into the temple grounds. The gate itself is usually raised and approached by a flight of steps. It is highly decorated on its outer surfaces and without ornamentation on

16. Mulyaningrum, "Bali."
17. Hardy and Jerobisonif, "Makna Simbolis *Kori Agung*."

its sheer, inner surfaces. The second gate is the *kori agung*, or *paduraksa*, a roofed gate placed in front of the entrance to the holiest part of the *pura* or temple. This structure is often heavily ornamented and, typically, the most arresting feature of the overall temple structure. Above the gate or door to this part of the temple is the Bhoma,[18] a carved face, characterized by large bulging eyes, flaring nostrils, an open mouth with gums showing, four large teeth that dominate the face, frequently accompanied with curved tusks and round, extended cheeks, each with a substantial circular aperture. Framing the face are two hands, each with four thick fingers that touch the fluted ears. The Bhoma is the fierce jungle god of Balinese and Hindu mythology whose task it is to frighten evil spirits and protect the holiest part of the temple. The Pura Tirta Empul is marked by each of these features: the tri-*mandala* design of sacred space, the *candi bentar* that leads to the first area of the temple, the *kori agung* or roofed gate or door that leads to the third and holist portion of the temple, and the Bhoma carved above the gate.

The Bhoma above the gateway to the *utama mandala* is present everywhere throughout the temples of Bali. Its function as protector of the temple is significant, for the Hinduism found in Bali incorporates ancestor worship and belief in evil spirits, monsters, and demons that can impact the health and social order of a community. Practices that relate to protecting oneself and one's family and community from evil are everywhere present in Bali, evidenced in daily rituals of feeding, worshiping, and placating the spirit world to maintain a balance between good and evil. The complex emotive import of the Bhoma face is well understood by the Balinese who are deeply immersed in this polytheistic spirit world.

The imperative of the Bhoma over the entrance to a Balinese shrine or temple renders its absence in the design of the Palisari Catholic Church remarkable. The architecture of the Palasari Church incorporates various features of traditional Balinese design, including the split-gate entrance preceded by a flight of stairs, and the front facade of the church, which is much influenced by the classical *kori agung* style. The incorporation of these architectural elements was, in fact, part of a broader process of contextualization and enculturation that includes Balinese dress, food, and dance as part of the religious experience in the Catholic community. The intent, of course, is to enable the Christian Catholic church in Palasari to be received as genuinely Balinese and the Christian faith accepted as part of

---

18. See "Ornamentation and Iconography," in Davison, *Balinese Architecture*, np.

the cultural and religious fabric of Bali, rather than as a colonial accretion. However, the architecture of the church does not include a Bhoma,[19] precisely because in the Christian faith there is no need of the image of a god to protect the faithful from malevolent gods while the church is gathered for worship.

The absence of the Bhoma in the Catholic church at Palasari holds enormous theological import and speaks to a key message of the angel to the shepherds at the time of the nativity. The angel proclaims the birth of the Lord Jesus and tells the shepherds that they need "fear not." For Christ, the incarnate son of God, enables the faithful to replace fear of the unknown, fear of malevolent spirits and evil, with the certainty of God's sustaining love, peace, and justice. All this is there is to be discerned by one who comprehends the religious significance of this religious architecture and its relevance to the social and religious context in which it is placed.

As Diasana Putra notes in her article on "The Balinese Palaces in Gianyar," ornamentation in Balinese religious architecture is not merely a matter of filling otherwise empty space; it has meaning, religious or social. This ornamentation can be classified according to four categories—flora, fauna, nature, and religion.[20] So, the Christian church at Palasari replaces the Bhoma above the entrance to the church with the image of a pelican—an image that has a long history in the Christian church. The pelican is a great fisher, and, in its massive pouch, it holds food caught to be digested for its own nourishment but also food to be held and provided for the nourishment of its young, which feed out of the mother's mouth. The bird is an image of Christ, the great fisher of men, who calls all the Christian faithful to be fishers of men. He is also the One who nourishes and sustains the church.

The incorporation of an image of a pelican above the entrance to the church in place of the image of Bhoma is a powerful theological statement. Tourists and travelers who come to the church ignorant of the meanings of traditional Balinese religious architecture may find the incorporation of various pieces of traditional Balinese architecture pleasing to the eye. But the theological significance of the absence of the Bhoma will be missed, as will the contrast between the two religious narratives suggested by the pelican image that replaces the Bhoma.

The discussion of each of these examples—Handel's *Guilio Cesare*, David's *The Intervention of the Sabine Women*, and the Bhoma of the Tirta

19. See Wayan, "Church Palasari."
20. Putra, "Balinese Palaces in Gianyar," 144.

Empul temple in conjunction with its absence in the Palasari Catholic Church—underlines the fact that artworks do not stand independent of their artistic context: that a knowledge of the work, its properties and compositional devices, along with its broader artistic and cultural context, is essential to receiving the work in a full and authentic manner. Artistic context is not merely an historical point of reference; it is the habitat of the work, complete with the baggage of the time, place, and artistic practice.

The relevance of context I have attempted to make plain. If audiences are ignorant of the musical and theatrical conventions of Baroque *opera seria*, their response to Handel's *Guilio Cesare*, given its apparent overall disregard for dramatic verisimilitude and the assignment of the role of Caesar to a soprano, for example, will likely be marked by confusion and dissatisfaction. And, as I have suggested, an observer ignorant of the plight of the Sabine women will miss the emotive force of the painting. Likewise, the one who encounters the Bhoma and fails to understand it as the face representing the protector of the holy place, guarding it from malevolent gods and spirits, will also miss the emotive force and the narrative implications of the sculpture.

INTUITIVE KNOWLEDGE AND EXPERIENCE OF ART

We have argued the point that knowledge of a work and its artistic context is critical to discern and discriminate with respect to the artistic and expressive qualities of a work. Typically, we think of acquiring knowledge by means of a process of seeking, receiving, and ordering relevant data. However, not all knowledge is acquired as a consequence of such a linear, cognitive process. Indeed, it seems that knowledge is sometimes acquired through a process that is intuitive and that somehow allows for what may be termed "immediate apprehension". This idea, of course, is a matter of significance for how we understand aesthetic experience and our approach to artworks.

In the philosophical community, the idea of intuition or immediate apprehension has a history that extends to Aristotle. The apprehension the intuitive faculty or intuitive mental process is said to afford has been variously understood as knowledge, sensation, and "mystical rapport," and understood to signify the absence of inference, justification, and thought.[21] The application of intuition to the experience of art, then, claims the

---

21. Rorty, "Intuition," 211.

possibility of the immediate apprehension of a work without the labor of the mind and the application of learned skills of analysis and criticism. The difficulty this poses is the assumption that, on the basis of intuitive experience, it is possible to make a legitimate aesthetic judgment of a work, despite an inability to give substantial critical reasons in support of one's belief.

Among those who propose that the apprehension of art falls within the domain of the intuitive is the French philosopher Jacques Maritain. In reference to the apprehension of the beautiful, Maritain argues that "the mind . . . , spared the least effort of abstraction, rejoices without labor and without discussion." He cites Aquinas in support of his position, referring specifically to Aquinas's discussion of perfect love as distinct from perfect knowledge. For perfect love is sufficient, says St. Thomas, "for a thing to be loved as it is seen to be in itself."[22] On this basis, Maritain develops the idea of love and apprehension of beauty without labor. Indeed, in his treatment of this question of the Scholastics and their understanding of apprehension of the world through the senses, Eco observes that Bonaventure privileged love over knowledge and reason in his treatment of the perception of beauty. For Bonaventure says, "The greatest pleasure is brought about, not by contemplation of sensible forms, but by love."[23]

But as previously noted in this volume, Aquinas ties the perception of beauty to knowledge and to reason, asserting that beauty, consisting in due proportion, "properly involves the notion of formal causes"[24] and therefore necessarily involves reason and the intellect. In Aquinas's thought, "the good, being what all things want is that in which the appetite comes to rest; whereas the beautiful is that in which the appetite comes to rest through contemplation or knowledge."[25] Eco notes that Aquinas specifies sight and hearing as *maxime cognoscitivi*—senses involved to the fullest extent with knowledge. The purpose of this description of the several senses, Eco suggests, is to underscore the intellectual nature of aesthetic knowledge.[26] As Eco notes, Aquinas makes provision for types of knowledge, including the "immediate contact between the senses and the sensible species or nature of an object"; however, there is in Thomistic thought no knowledge in

---

22. Maritain, *Art and Scholasticism*, 21.
23. Bonaventure, as cited in Eco, *Aesthetics of Thomas Aquinas*, 51.
24. Aquinas, as cited in Eco, *Aesthetics of Thomas Aquinas*, 57.
25. Aquinas, as cited in Eco, *Aesthetics of Thomas Aquinas*, 58.
26. Eco, *Aesthetics of Thomas Aquinas*, 58.

which the intellect is in direct contact with the sensible.²⁷ That is, in the mind of Aquinas, there appears to be no room for a knowledge that is the consequence of "the 'lightning' of intuition," as Eco puts it.²⁸ Clearly, Maritain, a foremost scholar of Aquinas working in the twentieth century, saw the matter differently.

In the eighteenth century, Bernard Bolzano, speaking of the role of intuition in the apprehension of the beautiful, argued that an object was called beautiful "if its mere consideration provides us with pleasure, a consideration which we carry out with such a facility that we need not in even a single case become conscious of this consideration."²⁹ In isolation, this text suggests agreement with Maritain's assertion that beauty is received without the interplay of the intellect. However, as the argument develops, it becomes evident that it is not at all Bolzano's intent to argue the absence of thought; indeed, he suggests that "the degree of pleasure afforded by considering something beautiful increases directly in proportion to the demands it makes on our intellectual powers."³⁰ In a discussion of Bolzano's theory of beauty, Peter McCormick offers a paraphrase of Bolzano's definition of the beautiful, which assists in reconciling the idea of intuition and the place of abstractive knowledge in the apprehension of a work:

> A beautiful object is one whose consideration by any person with developed intellectual powers results in pleasure. The basis of this pleasure is that it is neither too easy nor too difficult for such a person—who at the moment does not in fact take the trouble of reaching conceptual clarity in this matter, once some of the object's properties have been grasped—to form a concept that would eventually allow working out, through further consideration, the remaining perceptual properties of this object. At the moment, however, the readiness of the intellectual powers allows the individual to arrive at "a dark intuition."³¹

It is the "readiness of the intellectual powers" that makes this intuition possible. According to this view, intuitive understanding is not given to any and all, but to the "person with developed intellectual powers."

---

27. Eco, *Aesthetics of Thomas Aquinas*, 61–62.
28. Eco, *Aesthetics of Thomas Aquinas*, 62.
29. Bernard Bolzano, as cited in McCormick, *Modernity, Aesthetics*, 131.
30. Bernard Bolzano, as paraphrased in McCormick, *Modernity, Aesthetics*, 133.
31. Bernard Bolzano, as cited in McCormick, *Modernity, Aesthetics*, 133.

There are others who offer intuitionist accounts of knowledge, including Étienne Gilson, Henri Bergson, I. H. Fichte, and Bertrand Russell; however, an exploration of these arguments would necessitate a study of its own. It shall suffice for our present purposes to summarize several central difficulties with intuition theory. First, the intuitionist argument fails to explain how we shall distinguish between true and false intuitions, or it takes the position that all intuitions are true. If intuitions are either true or false but not always true, then there needs to be a basis for justifying intuitive knowledge. If what is claimed to be intuitive knowledge is true merely because it is my experience, then we encounter the difficulty of the justification of belief entirely on the basis of private experience.[32] Beardsley states his negative assessment of intuition as knowledge in this manner:

> In so far as something is believed intuitively, that is, because of an immediate feeling of truth, it is not yet knowledge, but a hypothesis to be investigated; and when it becomes knowledge it is something more than intuitive conviction.[33]

Despite the problems with intuition theory, it has provided a useful antidote to the influences of positivism and rationalism. Surely the scientist-philosopher Michael Polanyi is correct when he argues that we know more than we can say; that tacit, preconceptual information guides the formulation of questions; the construction of hypotheses; the ordering, interpreting, and synthesizing acts associated with perception. The particular problem that intuition theory raises, for me, at least, is not the idea that there are indeterminate mental products of our experience of art that are beneficial and ineffable, that is, knowable but not sayable (this argument is presented in various contexts by Harry Broudy and others).[34] Rather, the dilemma is this: popular arguments in favor of intuition too often rely upon acceptance of feeling as an adequate ground for ascribing artistic value. This constitutes a diminution rather than an extension of the range of cognition that is relevant to the apprehension of the art.

---

32. See Rorty, "Intuition," 211.

33. Beardsley, *Aesthetics*, 391.

34. Further to this point, as we will see in the discussion of the role of metaphor in musical experience (in ch. 5), musical meaning is not only intrinsic and extrinsic to the musical work but is constituted of both "objective," verifiable knowledge and a more subjective and ambiguous order of experience that is also important and central to the value we ascribe to music and musical experience.

SUMMARY

The joy born of a rich and mature aesthetic activity involves an act of the mind. Informed perception and contemplation are marked by an awareness of the artist's eye and a recreation of a more authentic voice than is permitted when the observer, passive and naïve, sees or hears with only the partial benefit of his or her senses. What we seek is an order of experience that yields a glimpse of another's world, which in turn restructures and refines, rather than merely extends our own.

Having said this, it is clear that, however refined our capacity for aesthetic perception may be, we do not always approach artworks in this intense and cognitively active manner; it is also obvious that a developed capacity for aesthetic perception in one area is not generally replicated in others. A person possessing the perceptual skills that yield a rich experience of Baroque painting may not possess the ability to respond to the music of Bach with anything like the same measure of sophistication. So, one who responds with a discriminating eye and mind to paintings of Cortona, Preti, and Giordano may hear the music of Bach primarily as the voice of his or her own emotions. Even the musical connoisseur rarely possesses the ability to receive with equal measure a broad range of music. This is simply to admit that our approach to artworks varies considerably from one art form to another, one historical period to another, one artist to another, and even from one occasion to another. For there are many occasions when we simply refuse to engage with a particular work, precisely because it demands too much of us. This does not refute the fact that a mature experience of a work draws deeply on the work's imaginative resources and demands much of the percipient. It is simply to recognize that, for many reasons, our interaction with artworks is often casual or fleeting. It may at times be emotionally intense but poorly informed; or it may be intellectually critical but emotionally barren. Each of these responses to art is immediately recognizable to us, for they are common in our experience. However, each time the genuine voice of the work sounds, it does so in conjunction with another's labor—the labor of the one who has, as it were, called it into being. In these contexts, at these moments, the work emerges from the raw materials of which it is constituted and is transformed into an imaginative construct by a recreative act of the mind.

It is precisely because the demands of recreating a work are great that our forays into the world of art are typically tentative and prematurely brought to an end. Such a journey ought to be viewed as a progressive attempt through numerous and repeated efforts to recover what was once known but as yet remains hidden to us. This "coming to know" may involve a very long process, but it is one that is rewarded by the fact that the riches of the work are not exhausted by our efforts. That knowledge of the work and all that pertains to the reception of the work is foundational in this enterprise is of no surprise to those who cherish the beautiful and who recognize that aesthetic experience of a mature order speaks to reason as well as the senses and involves both the emotive and cognitive domains.[35]

The reader familiar with the writing of T. S. Eliot will recall Eliot's use of "real" and "immediate experience" to signify that experience in which ordinary perception is transformed into the real or immediate and in which "reason, will and feeling all fulfil themselves."[36] Each is essential to the process that is fully human. His use of the phrase "immediate experience" ought not be misunderstood, however. A rich experience of a musical composition or any work of artistic consequence is rarely immediately achieved, as I have argued; for many such works are not immediately accessible. Eliot's notion of immediate experience is not to be confused with the romantic gurgling of Mr. Swann in Proust's *Remembrance of Things Past*: "But then at a certain moment, without being able to distinguish any clear outline, or give a name to what was pleasing him, suddenly enraptured, he had to grasp the phrase or harmony .... that had just been played and that had opened and expanded his soul."[37]

There is no intent here to negate the goodness of the sheer delight, pleasure, or even ecstasy derived from literary or musical experience. However, the exploration of feelings in the absence of the labor of thought is often the mark of dilettantism and shallow aesthetic experience. The entirety

---

35. Parenthetically, in reference to musical works, there needs to be stated the qualification that works that are closely aligned with the formal features of the musical vernacular often require less critical and conscious analysis to be received in an authentic manner. Copland's reference to African music and the rhythmic gift that permits unparalleled ingenuity in the spinning out of unequal metrical units in the unadorned rhythmic line, and in a polyrhythmic structure arrived at through the combining of strongly independent blocks of sound, speaks to the complexity of this music and the fact that it is received and performed in a manner that is subconscious and instinctive. Popular music tends always to be received in this immediate and unmediated manner, whereas art music is generally mediated by musical concepts and aspects of formal design that are not immediately recognizable to the listener. See Copland, *Music and Imagination*, 79–85.

36. Frye, *T. S. Eliot*, 44. Eliot's use of the terminology "real" and "immediate" reveals his indebtedness to F. H. Bradley.

37. Proust, *Remembrance of Things Past*, 227.

of the preceding argument is not intended as a denial of the significance of the emotive domain in musical experience or the experience of any other art form, though it explicitly rejects the idea that a feelingful and even empathetic response to the sensual elements of a work is sufficient of itself to permit a reasonable judgment of the work. Moreover, we have argued that cognitive functioning is, in fact, essential to a mature and authentic experience of a work of art and that as one attends to the formal properties of a work, notices and considers relationships among individual elements, questions the significance of one element as it stands in relation to another and the implications of such relations to the whole, an initial, subjective, feelingful response is transformed, and the percipient is able to embrace the work in a new way. This experience encompasses a measure of objectivity and analysis, creating opportunity for a heightened appreciation of the work, creative process, or performance.

To the medievals, *ars* was, first of all, perfect form framed in the mind. While there may be good reason to challenge the idea that the work is complete in the mind and only manufactured by the body, the essential place of cognition in art must be agreed upon, if the full range of virtues inherent in musical and other artistic experience is not to be lost. This is true of the observer or listener as well as the artist. For engagement with a work or artistic performance involves participation in the work, participation with the composer and performer in the construction of the aural or visual image. A mature, authentic experience of the artistic—often called aesthetic experience—is rarely intellectually or critically passive.

NOTES FOR THE CHURCH

Attentiveness and the Toil of Love

For those engaged in the Christian life, both in our devotion to Christ and to the vocation and work that is ours, the labor, discipline, and striving after spiritual fullness and indeed perfection that mark our existence are colored by our understanding and experience of God's love and mercy. These disciplines, as the psalmist says, are a burden made light. That is, when we engage in the discipline of contemplating Scripture, for example, we do so for love, for the love of God and in response to his limitless love for us. And in love, for love, the burden of the discipline is light. This is true, I believe, in some measure, for all we do out of love; for love enables and encourages us, even in the labor of study and discovery, which so often involves toil in advance of the prize. As we contemplate and labor over the beautiful to uncover what is there to be seen and heard, we recognize that we do this out of love. Our pursuit of and engagement with the beautiful is propelled by love and desire and is, ultimately, indeed readily, rewarded with joy and delight. In all of this, we have come to recognize the verity of Aquinas's theological assertion that the beautiful is linked in a profound sense with the good.

Both in our spiritual lives and in the intellectual engagements of daily existence (the two in fact are not truly separable), and certainly in our engagement with the beautiful, attentiveness is a necessary virtue. Its significance as a moral virtue is clear when, for example, the object of attention is the One who is beautiful beyond all that is beautiful, as Aquinas says of the risen Christ. However, it is also imperative as an intellectual virtue in our engagement with the beautiful, whether in music, poetry, literature, painting, or any of the arts, broadly understood. This virtue, like its spiritual cousin, I take to be rooted in love or motivated by love, for it is a discipline undertaken in pursuit of that which we deem to be both beautiful and good.

When we think of attentiveness as a moral virtue, we are drawn to the theological virtue of love, the primary direction of which is toward God as Creator of all that is and to his Son, Jesus. The central claim that the Jewish and Christian texts make on God's people is that they "love the Lord their God with all their hearts, all their minds, and all their strength" (see Deut 6:5 and Luke 10:27). This dramatic, all-encompassing love spoken of by the Deuteronomist and repeated by Jesus, is a love that "attends" to God as Creator, Sustainer, Redeemer, and Lover. This command, foremost among the laws given to Israel, is in response to the indifference, diffidence, and self-absorption of God's people—qualities and behaviours that insulated them from neighbors and isolated them from God. This problem is, of course, equally our problem, the dilemma of the contemporary church.

All this is simply to say that human experience, ancient and modern, has always found the discipline of attentiveness to be a challenge to the mind and spirit, notwithstanding the previous assertion that the burden is made light by the love of God. The monastic world in the Christian tradition has established rigorous structures that make provision for collective prayer and worship, and individual contemplation and study, in part to address the challenges of distraction and inattentiveness. Those of us outside the walls of such communities and orders find that we too construct patterns of focusing, constraining, and channelling our attention and desires.

What then are the markers of attentiveness? First, attentiveness requires a measure of isolation, that is, a psychological and emotional (if not physical) distancing from the surrounding material and mental environment. So, for example, to attend to the musical work and process at hand, the musician in a chamber rehearsal needs not to be distracted by the matter of catching the train home or by the high-pitched hum in a ceiling light in the rehearsal hall. This distancing of the stimuli and extraneous factors that press in upon us as we attempt to attend to a particular task is critical. It is precisely this isolation that painters and writers seek when they create studios in which to work. This space is not merely a place to contain the mess of the materials and detritus of craft but a private and particular space that enables imaginative work and concentrated labor. This is akin to the purposes of the walling of a garden: to create a private and personal space and to separate one's view from the horizon, for the horizon speaks of endless possibilities, ventures, tasks, and responsibilities that encumber, even if they delight the mind.

Second, attentiveness involves an act of the will—a willingness to narrow the field of interest and concern for a time. Often, as writers or musicians, we set aside a time and place to write or practice and find that our failure to accomplish the end we expect to achieve in that time is due to a failure of will. Oftentimes, we cannot or will not commit to the demands of the particular labor we have set before ourselves. For a writer to insist on the completion of five hundred words a day requires extraordinary discipline. The ideas aren't clear, the writing imprecise; I don't feel well; I need a walk to refresh my body and spirit. There is no limit to the objections that weaken and obstruct the will that attentiveness demands.

Third, attentiveness is aided by the demands of a worthy object or purpose. We are drawn to objects of our affection, whether it is a work we form and refine out of the materials of our craft or the work of another to which we attend. Love and desire make light work of the demands of attentiveness.

Attentiveness is a critical feature of the Christian life. We attend to the promptings of the Spirit of God in our relationships, and we attend to the particular demands of our work, whether that is the shaping of a musical phrase or crafting a rhyming couplet. Whatever the task, concentrated labor and intentionality are often the companions of attentiveness that require a genuine exertion of the will. But, thankfully, there are moments when attentiveness comes unbidden, seemingly unheralded, not born of

Formalism Revisited and Revised

planning and discipline but as the consequence of a joyful and immediate intimacy with what we have encountered and known as beauty or goodness. Whether surprised by the joy of its arriving or having labored to achieve the quiet attentiveness we seek, we are blessed and encouraged by the intimacy, intensity, and sense of timelessness that mark our engagement with that which is life-giving and good.

5

Metaphor and Musical Experience

INTRODUCTION

As suggested in the previous exploration of expression and signification theories, the record of interest and speculation concerning the reference of music to the nonmusical is long, if not always distinguished. Much that was written concerning the philosophy of music prior to this century is the work of those whose knowledge of music was modest and whose principal ambition was to construct a unified system of philosophical thought into which music and the rest of the arts could comfortably be placed. The fact that literature, music, painting, sculpture, and dance are constituted of different elements and constructed by means that demand different skills and disciplines has failed to deter many who continue to group these and other diverse art forms as if they were a homogeneous set and define the purposes and values of their various processes and products according to one or another philosophical monism. There are certainly many defensible reasons for considering these diverse artistic processes and products as a field of intellectual inquiry, but it is clear that much muddled thinking arises in philosophical aesthetics as a consequence of the failure to account for the immense diversity among the various arts: the distinct character of the many styles and genres within each art form and the particular character of each artwork. That most significant in the arts lies not in that which binds them but in that which causes them to stand as individual and distinct.

Having recorded this caution, we return to the perilous subject of music and its reference and proceed to address the difficult and contentious

Metaphor and Musical Experience

problem of whether musical compositions have, as Munroe Beardsley puts it, "a capacity to *mean*, as well as to *be*."[1] The central idea on which this chapter rests is that the process of constructing meaning of musical experience is in some ways akin to the process by which we construct meaning of metaphor. What follows, then, is an examination of the role of metaphor in music and musical experience for the purpose of exploring the manner in which meaning is constructed of musical experience.

With the dominance of formalist and positivist thought in musical scholarship over the past century, the debate over music and meaning that raged in the latter half of the nineteenth century between formalists and expressionists has largely subsided. Formalist thought, though as diverse in music as in literature, has—with some qualification—supported the negative thesis that music is not capable of expressing or otherwise communicating nonmusical meaning and endorsed the positive thesis that the principal value of music lies in its form, that is, in its musical structure, design, pattern, and quality of sound. The principal activity of music theorists is the exploration of compositional structure. In reference to the "characteristic failure" of analysts in this century, Joseph Kerman criticizes the preoccupation of analysis with the "autonomous structure" of individual works: "Their dogged concentration on internal relationships within the single work of art is ultimately subversive as far as any reasonably complete view of music is concerned."[2] Ostensibly, musicologists have been far more interested in the relation of one work to another and in the broad cultural and historical context in which music is made and experienced. However, if we might be permitted a further reference to Kerman, his analysis of modern musicological practice makes it clear that the principle focus of musicological studies has been more typically limited to the establishment of musical fact and text. His central criticism of musicological practice is precisely that it fails to account for "the meaning and value of art works."[3] That is, musicology is not centrally concerned with music criticism. The question of value and the connection between music and other human experience has been more evidently part of the domain of ethnomusicology, where the theorist or musicologist also functions as anthropologist, sociologist, philosopher, or psychologist. This work, though it has had an increasing influence on the range and nature of musicological research in

---

1. Beardlsey, *Aesthetics*, 320.
2. Kerman, *Contemplating Music*, 16.
3. Kerman, *Contemplating Music*, 16.

the recent past, has occurred and continues to operate on the fringes of what is still a conservative academic community.

The traditional assumption that language is the form or vehicle that lends expression to thoughts, ideas, and feelings has favored the idea of a conceptual opposition of form and content, where a meaning component is understood to exist as content, independent of language or any other media. This dualism has been foundational to much aesthetic theory that claims content for music and is the basis of expressionist theory of the eighteenth and nineteenth centuries. The formalist disposition has not only been to deny this form-content duality, which is now largely understood as an inappropriate model for understanding the structure of art and the relationship between form and meaning, but to deny the relevance and value of nonmusical image and meaning in musical experience. However, while musicologists have been largely prepared to ignore the relationship between music and meaning, the question has been continually of interest to many academics in the field of music education because of its relevance to the purposes and value of music education in public schooling. For insofar as music is understood to "contain" and communicate meaning, it is seen to transcend that which is merely ornamental and logically peripheral to the purposes of general education. Moreover, notwithstanding disinterest in the subject for much of the past century, the question of the meaning of music has reemerged with greater frequency in scholarly circles during the past several decades as a result of other intellectual and theoretical developments, including the revolution in the theory of meaning and the growing sense that formalist theory is unnecessarily reductionist in its account of the value of music and musical experience. In the previous chapter, we examined the emotion theory in music and various arguments concerning the relation of music to human emotion. In this essay, we look again beyond formalism and explore briefly the structure and purposes of metaphor in language and the role of metaphor in musical experience.

THE RELEVANCE OF METAPHOR TO MUSICAL EXPERIENCE

What relation and relevance has metaphor to musical experience? There are, as we shall see, several reasons for pursuing the subject of metaphor, beginning with the fact that metaphors of space, movement, texture, and form, among others, are essential to musical perception.[4] Second, metaphorical language has long been part of the standard musical lexicon of performers, composers, and conductors and has for a hundred and fifty years or more had a place in the musical score as a guide to performance. Last, and most significantly, as Roger Turangeau suggests, the study of metaphor may shed light on the manner in which ideas are organized: that is, how the mind connects experiences and builds relations between one idea, event, or feeling and another; how similarities, patterns, and illuminating connections are made; how meaning is constructed of complex and diverse data. An examination of metaphor promises to provide information concerning how the mind relates one thing to another.[5] While several models of metaphor are explored briefly, most attention is given to the interactionist model and the significance it holds in the exploration of the relation between music, thought, and feeling. The exploration of the nature of musical experience and the suggestion that the mind links experience of music with other experience is not to suggest that the better part of musical experience lies anywhere other than in the experience of the music. The joy of musical experience lies principally in music's sensuous qualities and in the attractiveness of its musical relations and structure to the mind—that is, in its peculiar and musical way of being. It is nonetheless clear that the mind, in I. A. Richards' words, is capable of connecting any two things in an infinite number of ways. This fact affects musical experience, and it is this process of connecting musical experience with other experience that concerns us here.

In *Emotion and Meaning in Music* (1956), Leonard Meyer begins his argument in support of a formalist theory, which articulates his view of the nature of the relationship of music to feeling by acknowledging that music has two types or modes of meaning: absolute meanings, those which arise from the structure of the work and its internal relationships; and referential meanings, those which are generally understood to be external to the work. The latter are seen to stand in relation to the experience of a work by analogy or association, such that x, a musical event, is somehow like or akin to y, where y is a psychological state, event, object, or idea. In some instances, it is said that the compositional structure refers in some way to such a psychological state, idea, or event. Meyer does say that absolute and referentialist meanings are not mutually exclusive, but, in making this point,

---

4. Scruton makes this point in *Aesthetics of Architecture*, 82–83.
5. Tourangeau, "Metaphor and Cognitive Structure," 14–15.

he accepts and supports the view that absolute meanings are possible. The difficulty with this idea is the necessity it creates for a "closed context of the musical work."[6] A brief consideration of the place of metaphorical fiction in musical perception is perhaps enough to suggest that there is reason to doubt that a closed and exclusively musical context is possible. Certainly, the role of figurative language in the musical lexicon that we shall now explore provides further ground for caution regarding this point. While it is true that many of these metaphorical terms have essentially fixed meanings, being "frozen" metaphors that have become to some extent an abbreviated way of communicating a technical or interpretive concept, once the place of metaphor is admitted in musical experience, it is not difficult to envision a role for metaphor that requires the listener or performer to supply the relevant terms that may be suggested by a work or passage. The question framed in this way is whether music may stand as a metaphor. To avoid leading the reader on, I shall anticipate the argument and commit myself to the position that music, of itself, is not a metaphor. However, it may, in some respects, function rather like metaphor. Moreover, there are certainly cognitive processes involved in interpreting and constructing meaning of metaphor that are equally significant to the process of interpreting musical experience.

A final introductory comment needs to be made concerning the use of the term *meaning* in this chapter. The focus of attention here is not musical meaning understood as defined content of musical form but meaning as a construct of musical experience: the result of cognitive processes, such as comparison, association, and transference; and the construction of particular mental images, where a musical event or quality is fused with thought or the memory of a separate event or feeling, where the one illuminates or informs the other, and where the two forge an indivisible complex with a fresh cognitive and emotive force, which is peculiar to itself.

METAPHOR AND MUSICAL PERCEPTION

The idea that the metaphorical application of various concepts in musical perception might suggest a more exhaustive analysis of the relation between music and metaphor was raised several decades ago by Roger Scruton. But before we proceed to do precisely that, let us recapitulate Scruton's argument concerning the place of metaphor in musical perception.

6. Meyer, *Emotion and Meaning*, 2.

Metaphor and Musical Experience

It is his point that the very basis of Western musical perception relies on a way of hearing and thinking about music that is guided by metaphors and involves the transfer of concepts not literally characteristic of music to musical perception. For example, it is common to speak of notes within a musical composition as being higher, lower, or on an identical plane with one another, thereby implying a spatial relation. It is, of course, the frequency of vibration that accounts for pitch: the greater the numerical value of the vibrations per second, the "higher" the pitch. No one pitch is in a physical sense higher or lower than another (apart from the obvious case, unimportant in this context, in which pitches are actually generated on different spatial planes—e.g., one at ground level and another on a balcony). Musical space, then, is not a scientific model to explain an acoustic phenomenon but a metaphorical construct that creates a fiction. Nonetheless, the fiction of musical space is fundamental to the manner in which music is perceived. Such fictions also govern our perception of movement and texture in music. It is common to speak and think of a musical line (another metaphorical image) or melody as progressing, ascending, or descending, its movement as angular, leaping, or fluid. In reference to tempo, the terms *adagio*, meaning "to walk slowly," and *andante*, a derivation of the verb *andare*, meaning "to go," are standard musical terms that give life to the perception that music not only exists but moves in time. Like the concept of musical space, the notion of motion in music is an illusion supported by the acceptance of a metaphor and the resulting transfer of the qualities of movement in life to movement in music. There is also the language of texture, a term literally applied to a woven fabric, for example, but also figuratively applied to musical structure, where various musical elements, such as types and numbers of timbres, are "woven" together. Clearly, the qualities of texture literally ascribed to a fabric are not materially present in music; they are qualities understood to be metaphorically exemplified in a work. Like the fictions of space and motion, the metaphor of texture is vital to the perception of music and an essential part of the interpretive framework that permits the composer, performer, and listener to confer significance and assign meaning to an abstract form.

These metaphors and others enable us to perceive an acoustical event as meaningful and expressive, to perceive an acoustical event as music rather than mere sound. Of course, the very word *form* is used in a metaphorical manner in a musical context, where it does not signify the shape of a body or any material thing but refers to the compositional structure of that which is immaterial. The figurative use of the term rests on the transfer of the term to that to which it is not literally applicable.

The metaphorical application of these various concepts in musical experience and their centrality to musical perception suggest the possibility of a more encompassing role for metaphor in musical experience. Certainly, the transference and association essential to the cognitive process of making meaning of metaphor seems relevant to the manner in which music is related to the rest of human experience.

METAPHOR AND MUSICAL TERMINOLOGY

In addition to the concepts of space, movement, and texture, metaphor plays a significant role in defining the compositional and expressive intent of the musical work. Much of the language found in musical scores functions as "frozen" metaphor, that is, as a substitute for technical or interpretive language that has a literal equivalent—where the figurative term functions as a form of shorthand. This usage is of little interest, apart from suggesting the possibility that such terms once had a genuine emotive significance and that other terms may yet sustain a more vigorous function. What is of greater interest is the use of language in musical scores that directs the performer to play or sing in a manner that will cause the music to evidence or suggest a particular psychological quality. Where a psychological quality is said to characterize a musical work or part of a work, there is metaphorical attribution, for, clearly, a musical work or performance cannot possess a psychological quality. This transference between one realm and another is, as we know, common in musical experience.

One of the lessons that awaits each young musician is the fact that a great number and variety of decisions concerning the treatment of musical components of the work are not explicitly addressed in the score. The delicate dynamic relationship between one note and the next, between one chord and the next, are not quantitatively or qualitatively specified in the score, for the notational system is not sufficiently complex or subtle to provide such information. Matters concerning tonal color, subtleties of articulation, balance, phrasing, and tempo stand as unresolved problems and unnamed obstacles. These lacunae occupy the lives of performers and conductors who seek to recreate a musical event by building upon the information provided in the musical score and responding to the imperatives evident to the discerning eye and mind. To the uninitiated, the score is only a skeleton that specifies pitches and their duration; voicings; and, in varying degrees of detail, tempo, dynamics, and types of articulation. To the musician, this information and these elements stand in relation to one another and suggest a world of musical possibilities. To the musically uninformed, the range of possibilities is rarely as extensive, and the musical imperatives are seldom obvious. In order to convey a more detailed sense of artistic intent, composers began in the early nineteenth century to augment the notational system with verbal cues. Of particular interest here is the metaphorical use of language to communicate interpretive intent and to relate music to moods or emotions. As directives for performance, terms such as *amoroso, gracefully, sweetly, plaintively, sorrowfully* are, of course, vague; yet they are found in abundance in the music of the nineteenth and early twentieth centuries. Given their obvious imprecision, we are led to ask why these terms have such a place in musical practice. A brief statement prescribing that certain notes be played with less bow length and increased pressure might be of greater value to the inexperienced string player than a metaphorical reference to "fire." However, some metaphorical terms encompass a range of factors, as the example *con fuoco* suggests. In such cases, metaphorical terminology is clearly employed, minimally at one level, because it is a succinct and vivid way of communicating musical intent. Inasmuch as many of these terms have a conventionally assigned meaning, they function largely as frozen metaphors, that is, metaphors that have literal equivalents and have lost the ambiguity and resonance of active metaphors.

While the convenience of the frozen metaphor is of some practical value to the musician as a succinct alternative to a set of technical terms, it is arguable that the prominent place of figurative language and allusion to psychological states in the musical score point to the more significant role of metaphor in music and musical experience and to the profound relation between music and the human emotions. Simply put, the use of image-laden words in musical scores and compositional titles provides a reference to that which is external to the work. Notwithstanding the famous disclaimer of Stravinsky, many composers have viewed their music as expressive of human emotion, a fact readily supported by the abundant usage of emotive language in scores where such language is obviously intended to suggest some similarity or relation between the music and an external event or state of mind. For our present purpose, various examples are provided in reference to Beethoven and Mahler.

Concerning the use of descriptive language used in the score, Beethoven is reputed to have said:

> As for the four chief speeds which are far from having the truth or the accuracy of the four chief winds, we could readily do without them. It is quite another matter with the words that indicate the character of the piece. These we cannot give up, for the tempo is more the body, while these refer to the soul of the piece itself.[7]

If Schindler's report is correct, it would seem that the depiction of the psychological and emotive character of the work by means of descriptive language placed in the score was accepted by Beethoven as reasonable and necessary. Schindler, an acquaintance and biographer of Beethoven, reinforces Beethoven's acceptance of the relation between music and emotion by relating the story of the composer's response to a question he, Schindler, posed concerning the interpretive "key" to sonatas op. 31 and 57. Beethoven is recorded as having directed Schindler to Shakespeare's *Tempest*,[8] suggesting that the two works shared an emotive quality and that knowledge of that quality in the play would lead to an understanding of it in the musical work. That music in some way represented states of mind, Beethoven accepted as reasonable and obvious. It was only surprising that, for some, it should seem necessary that the composer provide an interpretive key.

Mahler also spoke of the central place of emotion in music. In a letter (1893) to Gisella Tolney-Witt, he refers to the task of the composer to portray the "complex aspects of his emotional life." This reference occurs in the following context:

> In the course of time . . . [composers] have had such bad experiences that they began to concern themselves with making sure the performer had unambiguous directions as to their intentions. So, a great system of sign-language gradually evolved, which—like the heads of notes indicating pitch—provided a definite reference for duration or volume. Together with this, moreover, came the *appropriation of new elements of feeling* as objects of imitation in sounds—i.e. the composer began to relate ever deeper and more complex aspects of his emotional life to the area of his creativeness—until with Beethoven the *new era* of music began: from now on the *fundamentals* are no longer mood—that is to say, mere

---

7. Schindler, *Beethoven*, 423.
8. Schindler, *Beethoven*, 406.

sadness, etc.—but also the transition from one to the other—conflicts—physical nature and its effect on us—humour and poetic ideas—all these become objects of musical imitation.[9]

In 1902, Mahler writes:

> From Beethoven onwards there is no modern music that has not its inner programme. But any music about which one first has to tell the listener what experience it embodies, and what he is meant to experience, is worthless.[10]

Both of these texts comment on the composer's understanding of the fundamental relation between music and emotion: the music's "inner programme" is its reference to mood and emotion as well as to ideas and events in the natural world. Mahler's assertion that a programme is unnecessary to explain the music is essentially an argument for the self-sufficiency of a good musical work as a means of communication. That he took verbal cues in the score to be a vital part of communicating with the performer is obvious from the extensive use of text in his works; for example, *Das Lied von der Erde* (1908–1909), one of the last works of Mahler, includes an extensive range of terms intended to convey the emotive import of the music: among these (translated here into English) are the terms *mournful, cheerful, heartfelt, brazen, raw, shivering, caressing, tender, wild, musing,* and *nobly*.[11] It is also worth noting that Mahler included text as a means of clarifying the relation of the music to its emotional import in symphonies two, three, four, and eight. In the context of Mahler's compositions, metaphorical language in the score is purposefully used to direct the mind of the performer to the "spirit" or intended emotional character of the composition. Where the term does not function as a frozen metaphor (for example, words such as *musing, brazen,* and *raw*), the performer is expected to make appropriate judgments concerning its technical and musical implications. Mahler's point concerning the inferiority of music that requires explanation is taken. However, the frequent use of figurative language in his music and much of the music of the nineteenth and early twentieth centuries suggests that composers intended language to serve not only as a frozen metaphor, but as an active and resonant device for the purpose of commenting upon the character and expressive intent of the work.

---

9. Gustav Mahler, as cited in Martner, *Selected Letters*, 148.
10. Gustav Mahler, as cited in Martner, *Selected Letters*, 262.
11. Mahler, *Lied von der Erde*.

Beethoven, Mahler, and most romantic composers perceived the relationship between music and the emotions as an obvious and central feature of art. On this matter, they were in agreement with other artists and philosophers, for the prevalent disposition throughout the century was that music and the other arts constituted an outpouring and embodiment of human emotion. The articulate and forceful objections of Hanslick to expression theory and the assumption of a vital and necessary relationship between music and feeling represented a minority position. The common practice of composers, musicians, and music lovers was to link music and emotional experience and to ascribe value to music according to its expressive value. The increasing adoption of a formalist-structuralist perspective by composers and musical academics after World War I resulted in a philosophical schism between the learned and the broader population, which largely continued to hold a romantic, expressionist view.

As a point of departure, it is reasonable to state that some music and most romantic composition is intended to be expressive of human emotion or events external to the music. And, as Meyer suggests, it seems evident that many people, present and past, hear and experience music as signifying something beyond itself. I suspect, however, that our construction of meaning does not operate in such a way as to guarantee the separation of meaning that is "absolute" from that which is the result of recourse to ideas and events external to the music. Indeed, we may well ask whether absolute meaning, that which is only and purely derived from the musical structure, is possible. What follows is an examination of the structure of metaphor and an exploration of the manner in which metaphor is comprehended. Central to this discussion is the idea that the associative and connective functions of the mind are essential to its operation, such that nothing is perceived in a vacuum. As I. A. Richards argues, "The mind is capable of connecting any two things in an infinitely large number of ways. Which of these it chooses is settled with reference to some larger whole or aim."[12] The hope is that this exploration of metaphor will provide some insight concerning how meaning is constructed of musical experience.

---

12. Richards, *Philosophy of Rhetoric*, 125.

Metaphor and Musical Experience

THEORIES OF METAPHOR

The traditional grounds for explaining the structure of metaphor are comparison and substitution, proposed by Aristotle.[13] The essence of the comparison and substitution views is that metaphor involves a transference of features from one subject to another, the effect of which is the illumination of the one subject by the other. According to these views, metaphor is little more than simile without the use of "like" or "as." In the case of the metaphor "man is a wolf," the figurative structure compares the two subjects named and suggests that certain features—such as ferociousness and treacherousness—attributable to the latter be applied to the former. Critical to the substitution and comparison views is the notion that the metaphor communicates in a figurative manner that which could be expressed literally and explicitly. According to these theories, the value of metaphor is seen to lie in its decorative function and in the pleasure that results in solving a semantic puzzle.

In response to these traditional views of metaphor, I. A. Richards offers an account that speaks to the relationship between the two subjects juxtaposed in a metaphorical construct. In his view, metaphor as substitution accomplishes nothing other than the limited rhetorical objective of saying something that may be rendered in a straightforward and literal manner in a more colorful and pleasing way. While this model accounts for some instances of metaphor, he argues that it is incapable of explaining the more subtle ways in which metaphors, particularly complex and powerful metaphors, function. Rather than functioning as merely a colorful substitution for a plain rendering, Richards views metaphor as involving "a borrowing between and intercourse of thoughts, a transaction between contexts."[14] This argument claims a dynamic relation between the two subjects, which results in an "interillumination" of the subjects and an extension of meaning beyond that contained by either subject or the sum of the two subjects. The interaction model of Richards, since developed by Max Black and others, such as Paul Henle and Cleanth Brooks, involves what Allan Paivio terms "relational perception," a process of integration and "the perception of a new entity."[15] According to this view, metaphor is not merely the decorative substitution of one term for another but the creation

---

13 Aristotle, *Rhetoric*, III, iv, 1–3.
14. Richards, *Philosophy of Rhetoric*, 94.
15. Paivio, "Psychological Processes," 153.

of a new entity. Moreover, the construction of this new entity constitutes an extension of language—a verbal construct that cannot be restated without loss or redefinition, an image that has no literal equivalent.

The problem surrounding the idea that metaphor cannot be literally restated is commonly referred to as the "heresy of paraphrase." Cleanth Brooks speaks to the question of whether it is possible to provide a literal equivalent to a metaphor and suggests that "whatever statement we may seize upon as incorporating the 'meaning' of the poem, immediately the imagery and the rhythm seem to set up tensions with it, warping and twisting it, qualifying and revising it."[16] Like Max Black, he argues that a paraphrase can never capture the character and quality of the metaphorical image, for it says either too little or too much. Paul Henle locates the difficulty in translating metaphor in the multiple relations and similarities on which the figurative structure is based: "Many poetic metaphors are multiple iconic—there being not merely one basic similarity on which the metaphor is based but several. Each of these may be capable of indefinite expansion, and there may be interactions between the similarities."[17] The idea of the irreducibility of metaphor is essential to the interactionist view because of the premise that metaphor is not simply an ornamental device, a colorful or oblique manner of saying something that could be otherwise stated to the full and same effect. It is not merely a substitution of one term for another. It is, rather, an "irreducible cognitive force"—irreducible, in the sense that it cannot be discursively restated without loss.[18] If metaphor does not merely rely upon substitution or comparison as a basis for its functioning as a figurative device, then, clearly, substitution and comparison will not stand as adequate grounds for the interpretation of metaphor. The question remains, then, how is the conceptual and cognitive content of metaphor to be grasped? If metaphor is not translatable, how is it understood?

THE COMPREHENSION OF METAPHOR

It has been said that all translation involves transformation.[19] Northrop Frye once remarked, "Logically two things can never be the same and

---

16. Brooks, *Well Wrought Urn*, 161.
17. Henle, "Metaphor," 194.
18. Kittay, *Metaphor*, 37.
19. This argument, referred to as the "heresy of paraphrase," was vigorously argued by the New Critics. See Wimsatt, *Verbal Icon*, 3–20.

still remain two things."[20] So, he says, the poet's assertion that one thing is another, such as Shakespeare's claim "Thou that art now the world's fresh ornament / And only herald to the gaudy spring"[21] is both illogical and false. This is to say, the literal meaning of the text is false and illogical; it is the text as metaphorical construct that is meaningful. As Frye argues, the poet does not attempt to describe with scientific precision nor to develop a parallel or pictorial presentation in which A is a logical representation of B. The poem, as a poem, has no descriptive, literal meaning. Its meaning is not its literal "content," which is often false and illogical, as the Shakespearean example suggests, but its poetical meaning—a meaning that is "centripetal" or inward, variable, and vague. It is "incantation, a harmony of sounds and a sense of growing richness of meaning unlimited by denotation."[22] This "richness of meaning unlimited by denotation," this poetical meaning both vague and variable, may characterize metaphor as it may any other poetic device or structure. The literary response to a poem or metaphor is not to construct a literal or descriptive meaning, a translation or paraphrase; it is, rather, explication.

The vagueness and variability of poetical meaning is the result of various factors, including the multiple nuances and allusions that arise from a particular combination of words, the particular context in which the image or thought occurs, and the variability of meaning of the words that stand as composite elements of a poetical structure. With respect to the meaning of words, Terence Hawkes contends that the meaning of A is never fully stated in a single instance of its usage, for "A has a larger capacity to mean which derives from its particular context or use."[23] Where, in a particular usage, a word is released from its habitual referent, the possibility exists that the word may "combine with an enormous number of referents."[24] This reminds us of I. A. Richards's assertion referred to previously, regarding the mind's capacity to connect things in an unlimited number of ways. Further to the ambiguity of words and verbal structures, Christopher Norris, speaking of the "surpassing of structure by meaning" underscores the contribution of phenomenology, in its contradiction of structuralist thought and its emphasis on the "excess of the signified over the signifying." It is the fact of

20. Frye, *Educated Imagination*, 11.
21. William Shakespeare, "Sonnet 1."
22. Frye, *Educated Imagination and Other*, 139.
23. Hawkes, *Structuralism and Semiotics*, 64.
24. Hawkes, *Structuralism and Semiotics*, 64.

excess of the signified over the signifying that places metaphor beyond the reach of reductive explanations.[25] The question then arises how the reader identifies or constructs an appropriate meaning, given the ambiguity of the term, phrase, or thought as articulated.

Hawkes suggests that the reader selects from the range of meanings available on the basis of convention and on the basis of the "expectations aroused by the poem itself."[26] Clearly, apt and illuminating referents are largely selected by the reader on the basis of convention, knowledge of convention, and the capacity of the reader to construct meaning, which account for what Hawkes refers to as "the expectations" of the poem itself. Black makes a similar argument; he suggests readers derive meaning from a metaphorical construct, which, at a surface level, constitutes a logical absurdity, as a result of a shared cultural and historical tradition that provides a base of "associated commonplaces," something he defines as "a system of ideas, not sharply delineated, and yet sufficiently definite to admit of detailed enumeration."[27] According to this view, the effect of referring to man as a wolf is "to evoke the wolf-system of related commonplaces." Essential to Black's argument is the existence of an "allusionary" base shared by the author and reader; otherwise, the poetic intent and content of the metaphor are uninterpretable. Furthermore, the associations that are made rely upon historical usage, for it is by convention that we come to know that certain characteristics of the wolf are intended to be transferred to man and not others.

While the idea of "associated commonplaces" seems to have some value in explaining the manner in which some metaphors are interpreted, it does not appear to offer a satisfactory account of novel and more elliptical structures that rely less upon obvious and conventional substitution or transfer of elements from one subject to another. Janet Soskice, who offers an insightful assessment of Black's interaction theory and his assumption that metaphor has two subjects rather than one "underlying subject," concurs on the point that the efficacy of metaphor is dependent upon the hearer possessing a similar and sufficient set of associative commonplaces. What Black and Soskice underscore is the role of convention and enculturation as central features in the process of interpreting metaphor.

---

25. Norris, *Deconstruction*, 52–53.
26. Hawkes, *Structuralism and Semiotics*, 64.
27. Black, *Models and Metaphors*, 40–41.

Metaphor and Musical Experience

Central to the interpretation of metaphor is the assumption that nothing constructed of the human imagination exists which is independent of all else; there exists no free, uncaused, or uninfluenced thought or activity. Linguistic expression emerges from the experiences of the mind and body, which occur in a cultural and historical context; moreover, these artistic constructs are interpreted in a cultural and historical context. We perceive nothing in a vacuum; the mind, as an associative and connective organ, relates and connects sense data. As Chomsky suggests, the associative and connective capacity of the human mind is perhaps most powerfully evident in the construction of language, "'that marvellous invention' (in the words of the Port-Royal *Grammar*) 'by which we construct from twenty-five or thirty sounds an infinity of expressions, which, having no resemblance in themselves to what takes place in our minds, still enable us to let others know the secret of what we conceive and of all the various mental activities that we carry out.'"[28]

The character of an individual's interpretation of metaphor is dependent upon what that person brings to the work, including knowledge pertinent to the work, its style, and the compositional conventions upon which it relies and to which it refers. However, factors that influence the process by which one engages in "inference" and "conjecture," in making connections between the work observed and other works—and, more particularly, between the work, or at least one's experience of the work, and other forms of experience and knowledge—extend beyond formal analysis. The interpretive process also involves social, intellectual, psychological, and educational factors, which influence and shape the character of the individual's perception and interpretation of events; it is determined in part by the character of the individual's particular allusionary base—that storehouse of human experience used to construct points of meaningful reference. Accordingly, no one interpretive structure—taken in this expanded sense—is identical to another, for each emerges from a distinctive intellectual and psychological context. In each instance of encountering a poetic structure, the hearer's world is altered, and the understanding of the work remade in terms of his or her subjective experience of the work and knowledge of the world.

---

28. Chomksy, *Language and Mind*, 21.

MUSIC AND THE INTERACTIONIST MODEL

We have observed that metaphor involves the figurative use of terms without indication of their figurative character in contexts to which they are not literally applicable. In the case of the simple metaphor, the relation between the two juxtaposed subjects may be based upon an obvious similarity or resemblance; this is often the conspicuous feature of the so-called comparison or substitute form of metaphor. In the exploration of the role of metaphor in musical experience, we might readily conclude that there are many cases where a substitution model is to be found and cite references to things or events, such as Haydn's depiction of the "cheerful roaring" and "sudden leap" of the tiger, and the madrigalists' innumerable references to the cooing of birds and to sighs of love. Upon reflection, however, we are struck by the fact that this compositional device is merely ornamental and largely insignificant, rather like the lesser function of metaphor. Moreover, we are forced to admit that music is not metaphor, for metaphor is a linguistic construct, and music is clearly not language. This is not to say, however, that music is not akin to metaphor in some important ways, and it is this matter to which we turn.

Carl Hausman's study of interaction theory and its application to the verbal and nonverbal arts takes as its thesis the notion that the nonverbal arts are capable of functioning, like metaphor, as an extension of language. If "some instances of linguistic expression," in the form of metaphor and other types of constructs, create new meanings and references rather than merely make "explicit what was already there,"[29] then nonverbal forms may be seen to do the same. In Hausman's view, "non-representational works of art can somehow be fitting not only to something 'there' in the world but also to something individual and new."[30] While he admits that it is not possible to treat verbal and nonverbal image in the same manner, given the problem of reference, where there is no defined vocabulary and grammatical rules, he insists that both verbal and nonverbal elements may both "articulate significance." The use of the term *significance* is, of course, reminiscent of Suzanne Langer's distinction between meaning and import or significance, the latter terms used in view of the absence of specific reference. Concerning absolute music, Hausman, like Langer, sets its field of reference as human feelings and the life of the mind.

29. Hausman, *Metaphor and Art*, 30.
30. Hausman, *Metaphor and Art*, 167.

Metaphor and Musical Experience

In both Langer and Hausman, there arises the central problem of reference, for, as Eva Kittay remarks, "If metaphors are to have cognitive import, then presumably they should be able to refer."[31] It is precisely at the point of accommodating the problem of reference where Langer is most vulnerable. Music, she says, is an analogue of the sentient life; that is to say, the actual form of the music bears some direct relation to the form of feeling. Yet as a symbol of sentient life, it stands as "unconsummated symbol," or symbol without specific referent or a referent that cannot be named. In view of the absence of a referent that can be named, she declines to speak of musical meaning and speaks instead of import.[32] Unfortunately, the idea of music as an analogue of feeling raises as many questions as it is intended to resolve.

As a way forward, Hausman offers the suggestion that reference need not be understood only in its narrow sense of designation, that is, as the identification of "a single item or single and finite set of items." Referents, he suggests, may not be physical objects or objects existing in space and time: they may be "events," "moments," or "centers of relevance."[33] In the case of art, referents are "bound up with the work's qualities" and "immanent in the object," not "independent of the aesthetically apprehended work of art."[34] Yet, at the same time, the work "transcends its sign and is directed to what is extra-aesthetic and to what intrudes into the world."[35] The work, in his view, refers to something immanent in itself and, at the same time, is directed beyond itself to other experience. The idea of self-reference is notable, for where what is created is something new in human experience, the newly created entity functions as something other than a symbol of something that is already there.

The question of how the work as symbol is directed beyond itself and is comprehended as a symbol of something else is another matter. The answer Black, Soskice, and Hawkes give with respect to the construction of meaning of metaphor is that of convention and a shared system of ideas and images—an argument based upon the idea of enculturation. It would seem that the means by which the nonverbal arts are understood to refer, and the means by which appropriate association and transfer take place in

---

31. Kittay, *Metaphor*, 38.
32. See Langer, *Feeling and Form*, 29–32.
33. Hausman, *Metaphor and Art*, 93.
34. Hausman, *Metaphor and Art*, 164.
35. Hausman, *Metaphor and Art*, 165.

the interpretation and experience of music, painting, and sculpture, indeed, all the arts, is also based substantially upon convention and the knowledge and application of convention. We understand the use of a slow tempo and a modal harmonic and melodic structure as a means of communicating the plaintive quality of a "Kyrie Eleison." This quality of musical plaintiveness is not universally understood but understood in the context of a particular cultural practice; such comprehension rests, in part, upon the learned response of a conventional association between a musical structure of a particular sort and an emotional quality. As Black and Soskice suggest, making sense of the metaphorical image requires knowledge shared within a culture, shared by the poet and the reader, shared by the composer and the listener. This is what Black terms a "system of associated commonplaces." The meaning of metaphor, according to this view, is construed in a cultural and literary context, and each act of constructing meaning of metaphor requires that "the hearer must infer from the wider context what the speaker intends."[36] While the mystery of the efficacy of the powerful metaphor may lie in the juxtaposition of terms that have the force and freshness to create a rich and evocative image, it is seems altogether evident that the effectiveness of even a forceful and eloquent image is dependent upon the imaginative capacity of the reader to interpret the context and engage in the process of transference, association, and extension necessary to construct an appropriate meaning.

The point to be made is that the problem of reference in the construction of meaning is not unique to musical experience. The responsibility of the listener is not unlike that of the reader, where the listener takes into account anything other than the music as sound and form. Where nonmusical elements are introduced and invade the listener's musical experience, there is constructed a musical world that is no longer purely musical. Here, the listener makes connections and builds meaning dependent upon the images and texture of the mental life that are his or her own and that are deemed relevant.

In music, many of the conventional associations between the musical and the nonmusical stand as the result of the association of text and music or the association of music with religious ritual or other social functions. There is, of course, an extensive tradition of rhetorical device in music. These include the imitative practices referred to previously, by which composers reinforce the sounds of the lover's sigh by a falling interval; the bird's

---

36. Soskice, *Metaphor and Religious Language*, 85.

call; the disconsolate heart by contrapuntal and harmonic tensions; the rising melodic line accompanying the text that speaks of a soul or prayer rising heavenward; the slow, chordal and modal treatment of a funeral march; the use of a bright, major sonority for a heroic or majestic theme. This type of rhetorical function in music has a long history in Western music and is abundantly evidenced in the English and Italian madrigals of the sixteenth and seventeenth centuries, for example, and in the English anthem literature from the sixteenth century to the present. Once a particular semantic or emotive connection is established between a general idea or feeling and a compositional pattern as the result of accompanying explanatory text, the musical construct may evoke the idea or the emotive quality with only the assistance of the title of the movement or work and perhaps without the assistance of text whatsoever. In making connections between one work and another, between a given harmonic and rhythmic character and a nonmusical concept, listeners make judgments concerning the relation between music and the nonmusical world they inhabit and make their own.

In addition to structuring meaning on the basis of conventional association, both metaphor and music invite the cognitive processes of imagining, pretending, and reasoning by analogy. Verbrugge and McCarrell name these as processes pertinent to "the metaphoric speech act," which are "distinct from those engaged in accessing and verifying facts." Metaphor that is resonant and complex demands, they suggest, "a perception of resemblances by means of unconventional reshaping of identities."[37] It is the "perception of resemblances" between musical form and human emotive experience that grounds Suzanne Langer's concept of musical import. The precise nature of the relation between two things is, of course, undefined and unstateable: they are facts not subject to verification, as Verbrugge and McCarrell suggest.

Yet resemblance and analogy as grounds for reference often disappoint the knowledgeable musician, for, while music may convey movement and levels of energy and give rise to images of texture, balance and line, beginnings and endings, and qualities of progression and change, music is incapable of providing verifiable connections between itself and any other thing. Where these connections are not clearly attributable to convention or analogy, they are oftentimes the product of free play and imagining that take us beyond formal analysis. The musically naïve are, I suspect, more comfortable with the notion of the free play of pretending and imagining

---

37. Verbrugge and McCarrell, "Metaphoric Comprehension," 530.

being accorded a place in the process of constructing meaning of musical experience. It is my contention, however, that music may be experienced critically and at the same time perceived to stand in relation to or to be intertwined with some other thing.

Music does, at least in some instances of our experience, function in this referential sense, in which the nonmusical is summoned to our attention by the musical event. In such situations, there may stand before the mind two subjects, the music and that nonmusical event or emotion that it evokes in the listener. In this situation, the musical experience shares points of similarity with the experience of metaphor, where the interactionist model applies. As in the case of metaphor, one subject, the feeling or event, stands in relation to the other, in this case the music, by virtue of certain perceived qualities in the one that are attributable or purposefully associated with the other. The ground for the association of the music with certain emotive qualities, events, or concepts may result, as we have observed, from a conventional usage or analogy, or, as Verbrugge and McCarrell suggest, from the less constrained process of imagining and pretending.

There is, however, another more significant process that Janet Soskice suggests in relation to the meaning of metaphor. Her idea rests on the assumption that metaphor involves not two subjects but one—one underlying subject. The processes of transference and association, though factors in this model, are not central in the sense that A is taken as a reference to B, where A stands in relation to B by analogy or comparison. In the model Soskice offers, there is the forging of a new entity, where the one underlying subject is not descriptive of any other, preexisting thing or state but is newly created. There is, I suggest, a parallel musical process in which what is created is the product of a fusion of musical form, perceived sound, and thought and feeling imagined and remembered. This new meaning construct is a single entity—such as the experience of a particular musical aggression or a particular musical plaintiveness. It is complex yet not divisible into discrete components of form and content. As metaphor is not a metaphor of something else but is itself a unique and independent construct, so the experience of a music described here entails an imaginative event that is not "about" sadness or joy; it is, rather, a manifestation of a specific and unique musical joy, for which there is no parallel. There is no objective correlative that can be named. This event constitutes an extension of experience and meaning.

Metaphor and Musical Experience

What the study of metaphor offers is the suggestion that the associative, comparative, and interpretive processes foundational to metaphor are also essential to the construction of meaning of musical experience. Second, the "associated commonplaces" spoken of by Black, Soskice, and others are also significant in musical experience, not because music is a form of metaphor, but because it involves (in some instances) reference to other things or emotions, which are understood by convention and cultural practice. Music is not a "speaking" of one thing in terms suggestive of another (the definition Soskice offers of metaphor), but, as musical presentation, it may be suggestive of something else as a result of conventional association, textual reference, verbal cues in the title of the work or in the score as performance indications, and structural similarities between the musical event and the idea with which it is linked. More importantly, musical experience may involve the creation of a new entity, a fusion of the perceived sound and form, and of thought and feeling imagined and remembered.

Music is not language, nor is it an extension of language. It does not so much fill lexical gaps as create them.

CONCLUSION

In musical scholarship, the formalist position has not denied that referential meaning may constitute part of our response to music but has insisted that such experience or meaning contributes nothing to knowledge of the work; for this reason, it is of little interest to music theorists and to few musicologists. However, if the subject under consideration is the value of music and art in culture (which, as we have noted, has not been an important feature of research in music theory or musicology), it is a mistake to confuse the musically valuable and the value of music. While the principal subject of research in music theory and musicology is the musically valuable (traditionally viewed as Western art music), the scholarly interests of educators, anthropologists, and psychologists, for example, embrace both the musically valuable (though the range of music is generally more diverse) and the question of the value of music and art in contemporary society. So, educators ask whether music informs and influences our thoughts, attitudes, and feelings. Is the work, as Goodman says, remade in terms of the world and the world remade in terms of the work? It has been suggested here that the relation between music and other experience is significant and that other forms of experience, in particular, the experience of metaphor, shed light on how we construct meaning of musical experience.

The value of exploring metaphor as a means of informing the problem of music and meaning is suggested by the role of metaphor in musical perception—the ideas of musical movement, texture, space, and line—and the place of metaphorical language in the musical score and in musical discourse. Metaphor involves an interplay of ideas. Consideration of the role of metaphor in musical experience suggests that the processes of association, interpretation, transference, integration, and synthesis essential to the processing of metaphor underlies the human inclination to connect and integrate facts and to construct meaning and pattern; and it underlies the inclination to connect the experience of music with other experience. The problem of meaning in music, and in the arts more generally, is more constructively addressed when there is a focus on the processes of integration and synthesis in aesthetic experience—a process in which the life of the intellect and the senses are framed in a holistic manner. The common man sees little relevance of art and aesthetic experience to daily existence; the devotee of art is commonly plagued by the separation of aesthetic experience from the rest of ordinary life. In neither is there a profitable integration.

In this chapter, I have stated clearly that music is not metaphor, but the process of constructing meaning of music and meaning of metaphor are similar in several important ways. That is, there are several problems and processes common to the experience of metaphor and the experience of music. Concerning the resistance of abstraction to translation and reduction and the problem of attempting to construct a single, defined structure that stands as "the" meaning of an artwork, it has been argued that we construct a problem for which there is no solution—as a child might do in asking the color of the equator. When we seek a translation of musical meaning into language or a translation of an evocative metaphor into a prose equivalent, we fail to recognize that there simply is no discursive equivalent for either the poem or the *capriccio*. When we look for the meaning of a musical or literary work, we fail to understand that the work has no single meaning; we ignore or are ignorant of the plurality of meaning and the influence on the overall structure of a host of variable factors, some ambiguous and indeterminate, that are part of our private experience. There is also the problem of reference, which stands as an obstacle to the interpretation of the meaning of music and metaphor, for the interpretive field is not wide open. The task of the listener, like the reader, is not merely to dream and concoct images unrelated to the work, but to make appropriate and illuminating connections between the work and the world. For both the listener and the reader, an appropriate system of associative commonplaces and an established conventional practice are essential to recognizing the authorial voice. Music, in its cultural and historical context—I refer here to its history of style—provides by means of precedent and convention associations between music and the nonmusical world. Finally, the study of metaphor also brings to our attention the fact that the processes of association, comparison, transference, and integration that are foundational to the mechanics of the metaphorical function are also foundational to the operations of the mind and therefore essential to the process of constructing meaning of musical experience.

Music, then, is not metaphor but akin to metaphor. It is not a "speaking" of one thing in terms suggestive of another, but it is a musical presentation that can be suggestive of something else, which relies upon association and transference of ideas generated by the character of the musical event to other thought and feeling. It is a process governed by factors such as conventional association, textual reference (either past or present), verbal cues provided in the title of the musical work or as performance indications in the score, and the structural similarities of the event and the idea with which it is linked. Music is not, like metaphor, an extension of language. Rather, it is a substitute for language.

I suggest that as we consider an approach to the problem of musical meaning that rejects the singular place formalists have created for an "objective" and scientific approach to the question of meaning. We can learn to hear and comprehend music differently. It is possible to learn again to respond to music in terms of its musical properties and to place that set of understandings in a broader intellectual and emotive context. This process is one of relating, integrating, clarifying, illuminating, and interpreting: it is a process of structuring meaning, a primary activity of the imagination. It often involves what is sometimes called fancy, an activity where existing thoughts and materials are connected by association, one which Coleridge defines as "a mode of memory emancipated from the order of time and space."[38] Together, these various means contribute to a process of creating a unified perceptual field that is characterized not only by coherence and depth but subtlety and variance.

---

38. Coleridge, *Bibliographia Literaria*, 364.

The Arts and the Christian Life

In *The Use of Poetry and the Use of Criticism*, T. S. Eliot asks whether we should shun personal beliefs and convictions about life in order to read poetry, or whether we need distinguish between poet as poet and poet as preacher.[39] To "edit" in this way, he says, is to fall in "danger of seeking from poetry some illusory 'pure' enjoyment, of separating poetry from everything else in the world, and cheating yourself out of a great deal that poetry has to give to your development."[40] I suggest that Eliot's comment pertains to the manner in which we receive music. Where the principle of isolation is operative in musical experience, that is, where musical experience is separated from life experience, we cheat ourselves of much. For human experience and our expression of what we value take forms that are both explicit and implicit, subjective and objective, sensible and intelligible. The error lies in the assumption that in each conceptual opposition there is one privileged term.

NOTES FOR THE CHURCH

The mental process of associating one thing with another, making selective transference from one thing to another, is part of the fabric of our mental and psychological existence. The question here is what significance this may have for our lives as persons of Christian faith.

The use of metaphor is a means of building out into the world, of expanding one's framework for seeing and assessing reality. Frye tells us that the point of the poem is not to communicate a literal meaning, free from ambiguity, but rather to articulate a poetical meaning. It is "incantation," possessing a richness of meaning that is not fixed to a specific denotation. And so, he says, the appropriate response to a poem is not to construct a literal meaning or paraphrase but rather to explicate, to examine and consider in detail, to illuminate.

The nonverbal arts, according to Hausman, function like metaphor, as an extension of language. They can, he suggests, create or suggest new meaning and references. Like the poem, music and other nonverbal arts provide a meaning that is variable and vague, rather more like the incantation of which Frye speaks, which holds significance for the reader.

In the Christian life, we experience this sense of particular significance in our encounter with great music. We sense that there is more to

---

39. Eliot, *Use of Poetry*, 97.
40. Eliot, *Use of Poetry*, 98.

106

our experience than a purely formalist account of perception of structure accompanied by psychological responses of expectations that are either gratified, delayed, or denied. There is something of spiritual significance or "meaning" to be derived from this participation in the beautiful. What we experience as we engage with great art and the beautiful certainly involves a pleasure we gain from the formal properties of the work or composition. But what we experience extends beyond the structure and formal properties of the work itself. Here, we speak of the work pointing beyond itself or, in some measure, being about something beyond itself. A better way to express this is that the work is capable of suggestion and intimation. The music somehow intrudes into a different domain. In all this, there is the work of and mystery of the Spirit of God. For as Benedict XVI affirms, great art, through the eyes and ears of faith, leads us to an encounter with the divine. Great art becomes a manifestation of the glory of God.

So, in Christian experience, we find in the arts, in the beautiful, that which functions as symbol and is directed beyond itself. Black suggests that our capacity to make sense of the verbal metaphor, or, by extension, the suggestiveness of a nonverbal art form, is very likely based in shared knowledge within a culture, knowledge shared between poet and reader, composer and listener. As I have argued in this chapter, what is evident with respect to the interpretation of metaphor, or the particular connections we attach to our aural experience, is the fact that we are dependent upon our imaginative capacity and ability to engage in the transference and association necessary to construct appropriate meaning. But in terms of the spiritual life, one's capacity to make connections between artworks and the Divine requires more than imaginative capacity and awareness of what Black terms a "system of associated commonplaces." If the beautiful in art is to point beyond itself and connect to the Divine, we need have eyes and ears of faith.

T. S. Eliot asks whether we should shun personal beliefs and convictions in order to read poetry. His response is that such a forced separation would cause one to deny oneself of much that poetry has to offer. Indeed, as persons of Christian faith, we look to find images of Christ and hints of his grace and presence in works of beauty. It is both right and good that we should expect to encounter him in our engagement with both the verbal and nonverbal arts. The scriptures proclaim that "the heavens declare the glory of God"; and though they possess neither speech nor tongue, "yet their sound is gone out into all lands; and their words into the ends of the world" (Ps 19:1, 3). And so it is with all that is beautiful. For all beauty declares the glory of God. When we hear a great choral work of Bach, Palestrina, or Sweelink, and find in it the voice of joy, of sadness, sorrow, or longing, we may make connections with the poetic proclamations of joy we find in the psalms or with the sorrows or sufferings of Christ in his passion. We may make connections with our own spiritual experiences of longing and sorrow that have been part of our faith journey and are brought from memory into the present through an experience of music, poetry, or some feature of our collective worship. We may recall a yearning for God and his presence that we now associate with a biblical text such as Ps 42:1: "As the deer longs for flowing streams, so my soul longs for you, O God," or a stanza from a cherished poem: "Why, since you wounded / this heart, don't you heal it? / And why, since you stole it from me, do you leave it so, / and fail to carry off what you have stolen?"[41]

All of this is to say that music and all of the arts, insofar as they constitute the beautiful, are more than formal constructs. If indeed the beautiful in art is, at least in some instances, an *epiphaneia*, then it is, at least in such instances, not merely suggestive of the Divine but revelatory, a revelation of the glory of God.

To return to the idea that music may be construed as something akin to metaphor, it must be said that it is not a metaphor of something else. But as Soskice suggests, it is an independent construct, a manifestation that is inseparable from its unique musical form; and for those with eyes to see and ears to hear, it is bathed in the glory of God. Of greatest importance is this, that as a consequence of receiving the beautiful, we find that we are sometimes anointed with the joy of the Lord and caught up in the wonder of his glory and grace. Beauty manifests the glory of God, and, in responding to it, we share in it.

---

41. John of the Cross, *Spiritual Canticle*, 45.

6

Music and Imagination

INTRODUCTION

IN THIS CHAPTER, WE SHALL consider the role of the imagination in musical performance and in the process of listening to music. The chapter begins with a discussion of the musical score as a necessarily incomplete articulation of a musical construct envisioned by the composer and the role of the imagination in the performer's "realization" of the work. This process involves participation in an imaginary world, where through a creative and imaginative process, the performer as artist seeks to recover and reconstruct that which has gone before. This process involves both a struggle with technique and the materials of the medium, and the problem of constructing a detailed musical concept that the performer then seeks to realize. Both are part of this imaginative enterprise that constitutes the imaginative world of the performer.

Second, we shall look at the role of imagination in the activity of *musical listening*. This is underscored in this chapter precisely because it is often thought that musical listening simply means listening to music. But as many philosophers have noted, to look is not necessarily to see. Likewise, to listen is not necessarily to hear. And so, we explore the question of what it means to listen musically. But rather than beginning with the musical question, we shall take as a point of departure C. S. Lewis's discussion of what it means to read in a literary manner. This discussion will provide a foundation for an answer to the musical question, for both problems are grounded in the relation of the imagination to the artwork, whether the work is a poem, a piano sonata, or a painting. That is, the imagination plays an essential role in enabling the seer or hearer to participate in the work in an authentic manner. Such participation, to reclaim the term foundational to Aquinas's understanding of the Christian's engagement with the Divine and with beauty, involves inhabiting the work. That is, participation in the world of the work involves the cultivation of a partnership and collaboration with the artist, which enables a completion of the work. For what is a poem but marks on a page, a sign of the possible, until it is spoken into reality and perceived for what it is and what it can be? Likewise, the musical score is a sign pointing to a possibility, or a set of possibilities, that requires the thought and imagination, the critical and attentive engagement of another to complete the work.

THE MUSICAL WORK

Musical performance is a presentational process, a process in which the articulated and coherent idea of the composer represented in a notational construct comes to fruition because of the musical imagination and the cooperative activity of the performer or listener. The word fruition is used intentionally to imply that the work in notational form is not yet the final product of the composer's intent. Its end lies in an authentic realization. Here, the composer must rely on the performer, for it is the performer who lends the work its voice—a voice which of necessity is both that of composer and performer. The task of the performer, and that of the critically aware listener, is not merely one of translating the score into sound; that is, it is not merely a replicative function. (Those who have experience with translation of text, particularly poetic text, will appreciate the severe limitations of this analogy, for translation often demands far more than a literal or mechanistic process of substitution. To avoid a profound diminishment of the subtlety of rhythm, cadence, and rhyme, of the perspicuity of image, the translator seeks a literary approximation rather than an equivalency—an approximation that accommodates the demands of the new language and culture.) This process, whether literary or musical, whereby the performer "translates" the score, is itself creative and highly imaginative. It is a creative and imaginative process that guides the transition from idea to presentation, in which the latter conforms to both the self-evident and oblique demands of the former, where the interpretive structure is consistent with the logic and limits of the idea as represented in the score and the implications of a given style.

Having asserted that the work of the composer is in some sense incomplete, it is essential to distinguish this incompleteness from that which is merely tentative or provisional, for the substantial musical work is neither of these. Indeed, it is most frequently characterized by a conspicuous unity, complexity, and intensity: by the presence of a conceptual clarity, a structural clarity that is both logical and systematic, the presence of significant detail and conceptual development. With respect to these basic formal criteria, we recognize that many qualifications need to be made, particularly with respect to music in the twentieth and twenty-first centuries. During the three previous centuries, the compositional elements of musical artworks were structured in such a manner as to provide a compositional unity and coherence. These musical values were evident in the interrelated and interdependent nature of the musical elements that comprised the work: the work functioned and was understood to function as an organism. In this modern era, these values are not always understood in this way. That is, the work may be unified in some way and may have a logical structure, but the concept of an organic whole may be thoroughly irrelevant to the compositional design. With this qualification in mind, it can be said that the great majority of musical works throughout the history of Western music are characterized by a sense of logical and necessary progression—coherence—and of the essential place of each part within the whole and its contribution to the character of the whole. It is this logic of form—unity and coherence—this process of musical movement in time from a point of beginning to a point of conclusion, which itself is a logical consequent of the development of its musical elements—melody, harmony, rhythm, texture—that defines the musical work as an entity.

To return the problem of the generation of such a realization or instance of a work, it can be said that this process is rarely straightforward, for the musical work is not in any proper sense a work, in the sense of being an object. Similarly, dances and plays may constitute performance events but are not "things." Even though musical and dramatic works (these are examples, not an exhaustive set) exist only in this provisional sense, the term *work* persists not only as a short-hand for a more precise if awkward formulation such as Beardsley's "artkind instance,"[1] but because it is as-

---

1. Beardsley, *Aesthetic Point of View*, 285.

sumed the work exists as something akin to a universal or ideal, of which individual performances or renderings constitute instances.

According to this view, there are many performances that do not constitute genuine instances of the work they name. After a performance given by my chamber choir many years ago, a friend and fellow conductor greeted me after the performance and congratulated me on a musically refined and stimulating performance. He could not fail to express the opinion, however, that what I had offered was not altogether the work of Bach. His comment was based on the belief that the musical score is the notational representation of a musical idea: it is not merely a skeletal form of the intended work but a representation of the logical form of the work that enables the subtle and knowledgeable musician to create from the notated work—and from the musical and stylistic context provided by other compositions of the same genre and a similar compositional style—an instance of the work. According to this view, it is this construction of an authentic instance that is the principal responsibility of the performing artist, and it was in this regard that my friend was convinced that I had failed.

This judgment is based on what? It is based on the concept that a work is comprised of both constitutive and contingent elements. The determination of what constitutes its constitutive elements is based upon an analysis of the score and other scores relevant to the genre and style.[2] In this case, my friend was declaring his disagreement with my assumptions concerning what was constitutive and what was contingent. My work as conductor and interpreter may have been highly imaginative and entertaining, but the result, in his view, was not an authentic instance of Bach's composition.

Not any and all performance ventures constitute genuine instances of a musical composition. To qualify, the performance must account for the logical character of the work and the implications the structure holds for phrasing, dynamic structure, tone color, texture, tempi, rhythmic character, and other matters of interpretive significance. Roman Ingarden makes a similar point regarding the cocreative activity of artist and observer—or performer. But his notion of a reconstruction of the work "under the influence of suggestions coming from the work" is not quite right.[3] Certainly, he is quite correct in asserting that the work in notation—script or musical

---

2. It is on this point of determining what is constitutive and what is contingent in any given work that there is often much disagreement. See Goodman's discussion of constitutive and contingent properties of artworks in *Languages of Art*, 173, 209.

3. See Ingarden, "Artistic and Aesthetic Values," 40.

manuscript—is incomplete or, in his words, "contains within itself characteristic lacunae in definition, areas of indeterminateness."[4] What is problematic is the notion that the work provides only hints and suggestions about how it might be realized and completed in performance and the nature of the role ascribed to the performer or listener in relation to the work. The issue that arises centers on the extent to which the performer or listener is responsible for generating an instance of the work and what criteria must be satisfied for the performance to count as an instance of a particular work.

I would assert that the substantial musical work provides in its form and structure far more than mere suggestions regarding appropriate and necessary tempi, phrasing, articulation, and dynamic structure, among other things. The conclusion of the forty-three-measure introduction to the tonic theme of the first movement of the second Brahms symphony provides a useful example of such implicit compositional expectations. This entire segment functions as an extended upbeat or preparation for the tonic material: it is characterized by a slow harmonic rhythm and an extended section of dominant harmony. The section concludes with the three-note semitone motif—A, G#, A—offered by the bassoons and oboes over two measures. This extension of the motif constitutes a compositional retard; that is, the pace of the introductory material has been effectively slowed by the extension of each note of the motif to a value of two beats instead of one. To incorporate a substantial retard in tempo in addition to the effect of the compositional retard is to misunderstand the intent and effect of the compositional structure and render the cadence lugubrious. Moreover, in the same movement, the three-note motif heard in the winds in the nine measures preceding the introduction of the tonic theme—measures 35 to 43—occurs as an extended anacrusis. This quality of anacrusis suggests a reticence as the three-note slur is completed. It implies a gentle weighting of the third note of the motif and not an affirmation of the repeated note of the motif as if to signal closure. To signal closure by affirming the final note of the three-note motif is to demonstrate an ignorance of the function of the motif at this point in the composition and of the first forty-three measures of the composition.

As musicians and critics, we assess the musical value of a given performance in terms of the correlation of the performance to the musical imperatives—not mere suggestions—of the work. Failure to account for the

---

4. See Ingarden, "Artistic and Aesthetic Values," 40.

imperatives of the work found in the score or text results in a performance that is less than authentic.

Whatever position one takes with respect to the status of the score and the idea of the musical work, it can be agreed that the work of constructing or reconstructing a musical composition is complex, precisely because there exists in this world no preexistent work in the sense of a whole and completed structure; there are only instances of the work. The work as notation is always, to some extent, indeterminate and only fully realized and complete as an authentic instance or performance. And the authentic instance is one in which the performance conforms to the logical demands of the score. This realization or articulation of the work is always the product of a cognitive and highly imaginative enterprise. In reference to this matter, and speaking particularly about Monteverdi's operas, Nikolaus Harnoncourt, the brilliant Austrian conductor and pioneer of what we now see as the early music movement, argued that these operas are "autonomous as works of art and perfect in themselves, as are all great masterpieces; nothing need be improved or altered." Important to the argument I have presented here is his assertion, made in the same context, that "the work itself contains the key to its own realization."[5]

The study of music is not, then, primarily a study of humankind but a participation in and study of a distinctly human enterprise, an enterprise of the imagination that employs the senses. The relevance of the foregoing discussion to the philosophy and practice of music is that music-making, for both the performer and listener, is centrally an act of the imagination. For it is the imagination that enables us to gain admission to the musical world of the composer. Accordingly, it is essential that the performer be capable of functioning as a musical critic and that he or she be able to receive the work for what it is. Those who would receive the work and accept the integrity of the work must first direct their attention to the work and not to what it may be said to mean or express. As Richard Palmer suggests, "It is helpful to see the work not as an it that is at my disposal but as a thou who addresses me."[6]

When we consider the making of art and the imaginative experience this involves, we must not underestimate the profound resistance of the medium to artistry and the realization of an artistic product. That is, we must appreciate the fact that in the production of the artwork or instance, there is a resistance of the medium and a continual struggle for technical

---

5. Harnoncourt, *Musical Dialogue*, 36.
6. Palmer, *Hermeneutics*, 226–27.

refinement in the process of realizing a musical concept. The struggle of the performer, then, is both physical and mental, involving both technique and refinement of mental image; it involves the realization of a musical concept and the resolution of technical problems that stand as obstacles to actualizing the mental image in sound. For the artist and artisan, this process is both despised and treasured; it produces pain, fatigue, and irritation and offers at the same time pleasure, delight, and moments of great joy.

AESTHETIC EXPERIENCE AND IMAGINATION

The image of artworks as imaginative worlds is one I have used to elucidate several things: principally, the fact that, as the image of a world implies, the musical work possesses a coherence and unity that needs to be explored and experienced if the work is to be understood. Second, the work is comprehensive. That is, a musical work is itself a world, an imaginative construct rich in variety, image, theme, and detail. Rich in relationship, nuance, and musical allusion. But as I have said previously, it is possible to listen to music and yet fail to perceive the work as a musical world. That is, it is possible to listen and not hear. The question arises, then, "What is it to listen in a musical manner?" But in this context, I want to address a more focused question. I want to briefly explore the role of the imagination in the process of listening musically, for this process is an imaginative one.

As a point of departure, I wish to begin with what I take to be a parallel question, "What is it to read in a manner that is literary?" I expect that in addressing this problem and recalling the argument of C. S. Lewis concerning the nature of reading in a literary manner,[7] our purpose will be well served, for both literary and musical perception rest on the imperative that the percipient engage in a vital way with the work and in a manner that is imaginatively highly active.

It is accepted that a primary function of early schooling is to teach children to read. However, it is less commonly appreciated that the more complex and subtle purpose, the central and more educationally significant purpose, is to enable children to read in a manner that is literary. For the educational objective is not merely that children be taught to read only for the purpose of coping with the most basic expectations and demands of their society: paying bills, reading newspapers, comprehending street names and traffic signs. Presumably, reading is a fundamental part of

---

7. See Lewis, *Experiment in Criticism*.

schooling because it both accommodates and transcends these utilitarian concerns. One who reads fluently has access to information necessary to the comprehension, transmission, and generation of information and ideas vital to a culture, vital to science, technology, and commerce. But whether the subject is civil engineering or Russian literature, as soon as the mind begins to connect one fact or image with another, as soon as the processes of purposeful juxtaposition, transference, analysis, and synthesis have begun, the reader has introduced into the equation the operation of the human imagination. At this point, the mind reconfigures data, articulates and rearticulates problems, structures hypotheses and concepts, and begins to ascribe value. The human imagination takes our world as it is and suggests what it might become. This, of course, is one of the fundamental values of the literary process. It involves us in an imaginary world, a world of ideas, and interactions that demands an imaginative perception and participation in the work. It is this imaginative enterprise that is primary among the chief attributes of literary reading.

Foundational to reading in a literary manner is the process that Lewis terms *receiving* the work. This he distinguishes from what he terms *using* the work, the latter being characteristic of an unliterary approach to reading. This unliterary approach focuses not on the work but on the imaginings surrounding the work and the subjective emotions the work arouses. The focus of the unliterary reader, Lewis suggests, is on herself or himself, her own feelings and emotive response to the work; in this context, the work is not received for what it is nor is the attention of the reader fully directed to a discovery of what the work holds. In contrast, reading he characterizes as literary focuses on the work, its sensual qualities, its character and structure. In the first instance, the reader uses the object; in the second, the reader receives the object. It is not Lewis's point that the using of an artwork is in some way reprehensible but that such an approach to the work "leaves one outside the full experience of the work in question."[8]

The process of using—as distinct from receiving—an object for a particular pedagogical purpose is similar in one important way to the use of an object for amusement or in the play of a child. In both types of situations, the object is less the subject of scrutiny than a vehicle for something else. As Lewis notes, a child's teddy bear typically possesses certain general features that render it suitable for play, but a highly ornamented or artistic teddy may not be at all desirable to the child. For what she or he cherishes is that

---

8. Lewis, *Experiment in Criticism*, 26.

imaginative play of which the teddy is part. Quite clearly, the teddy is not the focus of the imaginative activity. It is a prop or a tool to another end.

In the case of the amusement of an adult, he or she might decline to view a particular film or listen to a particular work on a given occasion precisely because the work demands too much. What amusement often entails is exposure to a work or process that makes few demands of its own, one which permits, again as Lewis notes, attention to the "event," to the macrostructure, to the obvious but not in a manner that is genuinely compelling. And so, artworks often serve poorly as vehicles for cognitive lessons or for casual entertainment, precisely because their nature is compelling and draws the percipient who is willingly surrendered to its world too much into itself and away from the other purpose.

Underlying the idea of the significance of receiving the object is the assumption that the object is of value and that the recognition of the inherent value of some objects is important. However, Lewis's thrust is not that there exists some canon of literature that must be appreciated, but that, to be read in a literary manner, the work must be entered into for its own sake and for the sake of the world that it creates. Indeed, quite to the contrary of arguing the merits of a particular literary canon, Lewis makes the case that any work that is received in a genuine and literary manner must be a candidate as literature, for works that are worthless as literature, he argues, cannot be read in a literary manner. What the work holds that is of value is its imaginative structure: the world, full in its detail and rich in its image, that is conjured for our pleasure. It is a world to be entered and explored. It is a world present before us that offers an enrichment of our experience, should we enter it.

In this age, the teaching of literature is largely influenced by the social and psychological objectives of general education and the sociopolitical values of the time. It is valued for what it tells us about our human condition and the uses to which it may be put in the development of appropriate human and social perception and values. And while these values may be significant, they are not principally literary values. Indeed, we recognize that texts are selected that lead to the discussion of particular and approved themes; but we also understand that the discussion of themes often leads away from the work in question, and herein lies the difficulty. A work may take as its subject a significant theme, such as the immorality of the degradation of the poor, the manipulation and deceit of the innocent, or the pain of unrequited love, and its readers may explore this theme and benefit to some extent. But those who have read for the love of literature and who have been captivated by the world of a marvellous work know that it is not the particular theme, plot, or set of characters that make a work compelling. Indeed, the work based on a significant moral or ethical theme may be entirely devoid of literary value.

The power of the literary work lies in its manner of being or presentation, in the particularity of its construct. It is this that distinguishes one work from another more than any précis of plot can suggest. It is the richness of an image, the bounty of its allusion, the aptness of the relations or associative networks it suggests, its poignance, its perspicuity that mark and set it apart. The literary work that draws us into itself is one that creates images of a possible world, a world that has not yet been and, apart from itself, will never again exist. For its riches are unique and never to be replicated. Hence the certain sorrow a child feels at the conclusion of a book that fills him or her with wonder and that is received as a present and vital world. For, at its conclusion, the spell is broken, and that most highly treasured world is gone from her—at least until a further reading. That its particularity, its specific way of being, is the source of its great value is something a child of literary habit knows very well. That it is a very special story is the point, not merely that it is a story of a particular kind or subject matter. To speak to the child of theme and the work as an example of a particular literary genre will do little to assuage his or her sense of loss. For it is not talk *about* the work that will help but talk *of* the work—as much as any talk will help at all. It is the particular character and that character's world that is missed and longed for. And the longing is the plain result of the absence of something the child has grown to value—something that possessed the means to sustain and nurture the mind.

To educate the child with respect to literature entails encouraging the child to enjoy the work for the fascination it holds. This involves encouraging the child to move beyond the mere event to the characterization of the event. It is not just the event of a kidnap that Stevenson depicts that is enticing but the detail and nuance of its imaginative shape that beckons and grips the reader. It is a love of language, a love of image, and a cherishing of the imaginative life that is characteristic of a love of literature. And I suspect that a love of image and language comes not through a study of language and image but through the experience of it in literature and poetry. We taste and see. Seeing is not a function of social status nor is it primarily limited to those of extraordinary intellectual gift. It is a matter of engagement with the work, a matter of imaginatively entering and participating in another world.

It is noteworthy that Lewis suggests that one of the ways by which we can determine whether a work is artistically substantial is its capacity to attract and sustain this vital interest and connection with the reader. Essentially, his view is that if the work does not constitute an imaginative world of literary consequence, it will not be able to sustain a literary reading. It is the literary and musical world of imaginative riches in which we rejoice. This, of course, lies at the root of Lewis's famous *Narnia* tales, where the children discover a new and fabled land by climbing through a magic wardrobe. In these stories, there is a physical action and a particular place that leads to this new world. In reality, this action is one of engaging the imagination and participating in the world constructed in the work.

The implications for the experience and teaching of music are for the most part obvious. To begin, Lewis's idea of receiving the work, that is, of giving oneself to the work and inhabiting its imaginative world, is equally important to the experience of a musical work. By extension, I would argue that, in listening to a musical work, we need to give ourselves to the work, seek to inhabit this musical world. This process of inhabiting another world, a musical world, involves receiving the musical work in terms of its construct and conventions, receiving it in terms of what it is. It involves a process in which the listener is reconciled with the work and its compositional and expressive intent.

This is not merely an imaginative process given over to free association. Not any thought or just any imaginative enterprise will do. Rather, the imagination is exercised in conjunction with a knowledge of the imperatives of the work. It is not enough that the listener revel in the delightful sounds and permit the mind to wander freely. This type of "tone bath" is a form of using, not receiving, to recall Lewis's language. The imaginative engagement that receives the work is one in which the listener enters not his own imaginative world but the imaginative world of another—the world of the work before him. Participating in a musical world occurs at many levels: the one-time hearing, where the ears are open to receive all that can be taken in on a single occasion; the association and study of a lifetime; and everything in between. This hearing and rehearing is a process of perceiving contour of line, the shape of movements, the development of musical concepts, the interaction of musical elements, the mutation and transformation of musical ideas, the interrelation of texture, melody, harmony, dynamic, tone color, articulation.

Like the exploration of any complex world, the substantial musical work rewards repeated hearings and deeper exploration than the single hearing permits. Repeated hearing and analysis provide a heightened perception and the reward of pleasure that comes of hearing and appreciating what is there to be heard and discovered.

Moreover, the musical world of the work, while an individual and particular entity, is nonetheless related to other musical worlds. Such works do not exist in a vacuum. As the listener is captivated by the particularity of the one, he or she is simultaneously enchanted by its allusion to others. So, the process of comparison, contrast, and transference that is part of our interpretation of metaphor is also part of our participation in the musical event. The imaginative process, the delight of the mind taking flight, occurs in the receiving of another world. It is, as Lewis says, a process "impregnated with intelligence."[9]

SUMMARY

The transformation of the musical score into a musical event involves a creative act of the performer's imagination. This process of realizing the score is, as we have said, one of accounting for both the straightforward facts and the more subtle implications of the score. It involves constructing a musical whole that accounts for all the constitutive features of the work, and it also addresses its contingent features. For the conductor, this involves developing an interpretive structure, a plan or concept of the entire work that accounts for all the details and variations of tempo, dynamic, balance, blend, articulation, and phrasing; a plan or sound image that is coherent and that is sustained by the structure of the work—by its melodic, harmonic, rhythmic structures; by its texture, instrumentation, and tonal relationships. While the significance of musical factors varies from one composition to another, and from one type of composition to another—piano trio, Lieder, symphony, opera—in every musical context, the performer, or conductor and performer, must construct a musical event from a notated source that is necessarily incomplete. In general, only the basic facts concerning pitch, tempo, dynamic, and articulation are explicitly given. The work that remains in the construction of an aural image of the musical whole is a

---

9. Lewis, *Experiment in Criticism*, 24.

process of the imagination informed by a knowledge of the work—both the work's structure and the musical conventions of the genre.

For the listener, the aesthetic process is also highly imaginative. It is one of participating in a unique musical world where he or she strives to comprehend the musical significance of the many aspects of the event. This interpretive, analytical process involves understanding what there is to be heard. It involves seeing and hearing patterns and relationships that constitute the specific musical process. For the work is a process of ordered sound. These sounds have a musical significance related to the work's musical properties. This uncovering of structure and internal meaning is an act of the imagination. Even where there are critical commentaries to assist the listener, the process of making sense of a musical performance and ascribing value to the various features of a musical event involve an act of the imagination.

Both the artistic and the aesthetic involve inhabiting a musical world that exists not in the time and space of ordinary experience. Our participation in the musically beautiful takes us beyond the routine and ordinary to worlds that are sometimes sublime. Experience suggests that participation in such imaginative worlds and imaginative process provides us with much pleasure. This imaginative engagement is surely one of the pure pleasures we experience. Here, the mind takes flight. Here, there is revelation and reconciliation, transformation, and transfiguration: the revelation of a compositional order, and a reconciliation of performer and listener with the work as they come to comprehend and apprehend its particular way of being, as they participate in this world and cooperate in its rearticulation. Here, it is possible to participate in the transformation of the work from its notated form to a musical event in time and place.

NOTES FOR THE CHURCH

The revelation and reconciliation spoken of above refer to the musical work and the relation between the work and the performer or listener. But the apprehension and the practice of art and artfulness, the imaginative indwelling of an artistic world, holds an even greater promise. This "transfiguration of the commonplace"[10] that leads us out of time and place offers, in fact, a measure of liberty, a means by which the often harsh and dark realities of the present are transfigured, and where joy is our temporary reward for participation in the artful. The capacity for artfulness and the

---

10. Phrase borrowed from Danto, *Transfiguration of the Commonplace*.

capacity for taking pleasure in the artful and beautiful for their own sake is a gift of God to humanity. The sons of toil and the privileged alike possess this capacity for creative and imaginative enterprise and its potential for empowerment and release, an empowerment that comes of the recognition of the merits of an authentic and joyful engagement with that which is fecund and artful. However, this transformation of the commonplace is not merely a matter of escape from drudgery and the routine of the ordinary. It is not so much flight from as movement toward: movement toward that which is whole, that which is beautiful and good. For the faithful who seek and see God in all that is blessed, this movement toward the work in its fullness is also a movement toward the holy, toward an encounter with the blessed One who is the light that lightens the darkness, the bread of life who feeds the hungry, the lover of our souls who comforts and embraces us in our want and distress.

I do not speak of fullness nor completion. There is no fullness here. The joy and happiness that is ours through this imaginative participation in the beautiful and the good is imperfect. It is a foreshadowing of the promise of God, the coming again of Christ, and his establishment of a kingdom in which there will be no tears, no pain, and no injustice; a kingdom in which beauty, truth, and goodness shall reign, and where we shall witness the full glory of Christ our Lord. Until the time of that fulfilment, let all who may, find earthly joy and peace in the grace extended to us through the beautiful and the good found in artistry and the artful, in the making and apprehension of that which is beautiful, good, and worthy; and may the church in its glory—and in its sometime vainglory—the poor in the midst of their deep poverty, and all humanity in the weakness of flesh, find an abundance of joy in Christ Jesus, in his creation, and in his gift to humanity of the capacity to perceive with wonder and create with joy.

This is a vital part of the *shalom* that we can and ought to strive for in this present time—a time that so often is marked by an absence of peace and well-being. But as we choose to participate in the will and ways of God, in the goodness of right relationships, and the nurturing of our souls and minds on that which is beautiful, good, and true, we discover that God has made it possible for us to flourish and experience joy even now, even amid the sorrows and profound challenges of a fallen world. A. M. Coates, in his reading of Nicholas Wolterstorff, makes the point that "shalom is not just peace, but flourishing, flourishing in all dimensions of our existence—in our relation to God, in our relation to our fellow human beings, in our relation to ourselves, in our relation to creation in general." Coates also makes the point that Wolterstorff links flourishing with enjoyment: "To dwell in shalom is to enjoy living before God, to enjoy living in one's physical surroundings, to enjoy living with one's fellows, to enjoy life with oneself."[11] To experience joy and delight in the good things of God is part of what it is to participate in the life of Christ and to give witness to the goodness and glory of God. This includes the delight taken in the magnificence of the created order and in the beauty of the handiwork of artists and artisans. All of this is part of the bounty we experience as a consequence of God's caring and provision for us.

This leads us to the final chapter and the subject of beauty and *shalom*—*shalom* understood as peace and well-being but also as harmony, wholeness, and tranquility. It speaks of a state of being marked by goodness and delight taken in goodness and beauty. For we are created in God's image to be bearers of God's image to the nations. This commission certainly involves proclamation of the good news of Christ, but it also involves giving evidence of new life, of transformation of heart and mind in our very way of being. This transformed state of being is marked in various ways, according to the biblical text. Saint Paul (Gal 5) speaks of these features of the new creature in terms of "fruits of the Spirit." That is, we shall be known as persons whose attributes are those of love, joy, and peace—among others, including kindness, patience, gentleness, generosity, faithfulness, and self-control. This goodness of character provides evidence of the Spirit of God residing in us. It is this Spirit who makes possible a life of love rather than a life of fear, a life grounded in peace and abundance rather than a life diminished by the limitations and inclinations of our carnal natures and the evil that so often afflicts us. The abundance that marks this being-in-Christ in some sense mirrors the extravagance, beauty, and goodness of God's created world.

This *shalom*, in its embrace of the person and ways of Christ, is marked by joy, gratitude, service to others, and self-giving. Herein is a "relational flourishing"[12] that marks *shalom* and embraces beauty "not simply as a property or attribute, but as a mode of existence, a way of being, a relational category."[13]

---

11. Coates, "Beauty Lived towards Shalom," 10. Coates references an argument in Nicholas Wolterstorff, *Hearing the Call: Liturgy, Justice, Church, and World*, 110.

12. Coates, "Beauty Lived towards Shalom," 103.

13. Coates, "Beauty Lived towards Shalom," 103.

7

ART, BEAUTY, AND THE CHRISTIAN LIFE

INTRODUCTION

WE BEGAN THIS VOLUME with a discussion of the Christian self and both the desire and responsibility to become more than we now are. I have argued that the process of becoming more fully human is part of our calling as persons of Christian faith, a process that involves a transformation of mind and spirit by which we are to become more like Christ. This process, I believe, embraces all of our being, all of who we are. As persons created in God's image, we have both the capacity of mind and the senses to understand and appreciate the virtues of truth, goodness, and beauty. As persons of Christian faith, we embrace and, indeed, we long for that which is true, that which is good, and that which is beautiful, for these are properties of God and qualities of being and personhood that are essential to our identity as the people of God.

In this concluding chapter, I begin by reiterating the proposition that the enrichment and fulfilment of human experience is a vital concern of all people; and certainly, artistic and aesthetic experience, that is, experience of the beautiful, ought to be viewed not as a casual distraction or mere ornament to life but as a critical part of an abundant life, and life well lived. The joy, wonder, and contentment that participation in these rich and complex imaginative worlds provide is evidence of the fact that participation in the beautiful constitutes a mode of human goodness. The hope expressed here for the Christian church and for persons of Christian faith is that we both come to a place where we are able to articulate more clearly the contribution of music and the various other arts in the Christian life and see this enrichment of the human person as part of a seamless whole in which the Christian becomes more like Christ.

A theological understanding of the arts and their contribution to human experience and the Christian life rests on the biblical assertion that the human species is in fact created in God's image and, as a consequence, possesses the capacity of mind and imagination for reason, fancy, memory, and the construction of that which is newborn; that is, for creation, not *ex nihilo*, as God has created out of nothing, but creation as an act of the human imagination by which the new is created out of that which is already known. Moreover, engagement with products of the human imagination and spirit generated by others holds the promise of encouraging a richer and fuller understanding of ourselves and the nature of our humanity. It holds the promise of enabling the maturation of the human spirit, of the transformation of hearts and minds in the process of becoming more than we now are. More importantly, this theological reading provides an understanding of the arts as a means by which we may encounter the Divine. For where the arts constitute the beautiful, we see them aligned with the good and the true, and with the very source of all that is beautiful, good, and true—with the One who is himself beautiful beyond all that is beautiful. In this sense, the beautiful may function as something akin to a portal through which we may glimpse, however indirectly and partially, the beauty and glory of the Lord.

How is it, then, that the arts provide a means of encounter with the Divine? As persons of Christian faith, we discover as we engage with the beautiful that it points us to God, to the source of the beautiful. As Balthasar puts it, "Everything of beauty found in the world (and with it too the true and the good) is drawn up into a relationship . . . where the living God is glorified as he pours out his limitless love for the creature."[1] This aesthetic engagement, this engagement with the beautiful, holds a significant spiritual value inasmuch as it enables, for those with eyes to see and ears to hear, engagement with the spirit of God. This interaction with the beautiful, and the part it plays in one's life and, ultimately, one's encounter with and knowledge of God, is part of the fullness and wholeness of the person that God desires for us. This movement toward wholeness is part of what is intended for us in our being-in-the-world as we embrace the *shalom* of God. Now, I have qualified this function of art as a portal to the Divine,

---

1. Balthasar, *The Glory of the Lord*, 1:12.

using the phrase "for those with eyes to see and ears to hear," to underscore the fact that not everyone who engages with the beautiful encounters God. In fact, most people who visit galleries, attend concerts, and explore the magnificence of the created world do not report a connection between engagement with beauty and an experience of God. This is ultimately part of the mystery of faith and the work of the Spirit of God. The theology of the Christian church teaches that we are not somehow transformed by the beautiful but by Christ. Moreover, it is the work of the Spirit of God that links beauty, truth, and goodness to God. The reflection of the beauty of God in his created world and in the beautiful products of the human imagination is seen by the light of faith.

THE CONTRIBUTION OF BEAUTY TO *SHALOM*

Let us explore further the idea of *shalom* and the contribution of the beautiful to the peace and wholeness that God desires for us. In particular, I want to focus on three ways in which engagement with the beautiful plays a part in the peace of *shalom*: first, we address the significance of the beautiful in relation to Christian hope, and the importance of hope in the life of the church and in the community and spirit of *shalom*; second, we consider the matter of the giving of gifts, specifically, the giving of the beautiful, and the significance of such acts in the Christian life and in the life of the Christian church. Third, we conclude with a brief treatment of the idea of integrity and self-giving in one's craft as an act of faithfulness, which is also a feature characteristic of *shalom*.

The term *shalom* is found frequently throughout the Old Testament, referring to peace. The term does not, in fact, speak about inner peace; it has, rather, a range of meaning that embraces the idea of peace with God and peace between people, as well as the idea of good health, favor, rest, and a general well-being. In its comprehensive sense, *shalom* can be said to mean a wholeness and goodness, a flourishing of the people of God. Psalm 85: 9–12 speaks of *shalom* in this manner: "Surely his salvation is at hand for those who fear him, that his glory may dwell in our land. Steadfast love and faithfulness will meet; righteousness and peace will kiss each other. Faithfulness will spring up from the ground, and righteousness will look down from the sky. The Lord will give what is good, and our land will yield its increase." This psalm speaks of the restoration of peace and wholeness. Where *shalom* is experienced, people encounter the deliverance of

God—deliverance from brokenness of all sorts, including deliverance from foes, from the corruption and degradation that are the consequence of poor habits, and from the proclivities of the carnal self. In *shalom*, one finds the commitment of God to his people, and the commitment of persons to each other and to the welfare of the community; one finds righteousness and truthfulness rather than lies and illusions; faithfulness rather than the faithlessness of infidelity, inconstancy, falsity, disloyalty, and deceitfulness. In *shalom*, one finds wellness and a wholeness that includes all facets of human existence—its physical, psychological, spiritual, and social domains. Where the Spirit of God blesses his people with *shalom*, we find people seeking to be in right relationship with God and with each other. The peace of *shalom* encompasses the idea of a right relationship with God and with others, and it also encompasses the broader and more inclusive concept of wholeness that includes the idea of peace and prosperity, as well as a general sense of flourishing. This is the comprehensive peace that God intends for us. It is the peace and flourishing that Christ will restore in fullness when he returns. But it is also the peace that God desires for his people in this present age. Indeed, the magnificent prophetic text of Isaiah 9:6 tells of the birth of Jesus who will be the Prince of Peace, who will be our peace:

> For a child has been born for us, a son given to us;
> authority rests upon his shoulders; and he is named
> Wonderful Counselor, Mighty God, Everlasting Father,
> Prince of Peace.

Jesus, the Prince of *Shalom*, brings peace in the new Jerusalem but also now, in the present age of the coming of the kingdom of God. It is a peace which is as yet imperfect and will be so until his coming again, but, nonetheless, this peace in all its forms is a mark of *shalom* and the promise of God regarding what shall yet be.

As the community of Christian faith, we recognize and affirm that the flourishing of the heart and mind that is characteristic of the *shalom* of God embraces the beautiful, the source of which is always divine. Indeed, the cultivation and contemplation of the beautiful is part of human flourishing. It is that in which we quite appropriately take pleasure and delight, for beauty is a gift of God. Moreover, the beautiful, both the product of the human imagination and the superabundant beauty of creation, reflects God's glory and infinite goodness. The beauty of the earth, the beauty of God's creatures, and the beauty of mind—this profusion of beauty is evidence of the great goodness and faithfulness of God toward us and contributes to the wholeness and flourishing of God's people.

SHALOM: BEAUTY AND CHRISTIAN HOPE

In previous chapters, we have spoken of art and its value in terms of beauty, significant form, and various modes of expression of human emotion. At this point, I want to return to the idea of the beautiful and present the case that artworks, understood as instances of the beautiful, are important, because they are, in a sense, newborn and transformative, and because they nurture Christian hope.

We typically think of the beautiful in art as not merely replicative of that which is but something novel, something newborn, the imaginative product of the human mind. In this sense, it mirrors, albeit in a profoundly partial and temporal manner, God's work in creation. In some theological circles, there is considerable reservation concerning use of the term *create* in relation to human artistic enterprise, given that only God creates *ex nihilo*. What artists and artisans do is construct things out of existing materials. We do not create out of nothing. With this caveat in mind, we proceed with the term *create* in a qualified manner.

Now, with respect to these newly created things, one recognizes that they may certainly follow a model or preexisting form or genre. A violin concerto, for example, may well be comprised of three movements, with the typical structure of a double exposition—the first for the orchestra, independent of the soloist; and the second sustained principally by the soloist, during which the material modulates into a related and contrasting key. Nonetheless, within the category of concerto form, a newly composed work is newborn in the sense that the material, its combination of melodic, harmonic, and rhythmic ideas, is uniquely combined and structured. Such a work constitutes an instance of new growth, a new thing added to the existing musical literature. This new growth, though certainly not unique to the Christian community, is part of the fecundity that the human community experiences as a consequence of humanity having been created in God's image. This abundance of new growth, new instances of the beautiful, contributes to the flowering of the kingdom of God and our experience, as Christians, of the peace and flourishing that is ours in Christ.

Second, as this new thing is experienced, we recognize that the present is transformed, for this new world takes us beyond the rivulets of daily life and makes possible a participation in and contemplation of the beautiful. In the language of Aquinas and the Scholastics, participation in the beautiful involves participation in the good, and as we participate in and engage with the beautiful in music, poetry, or painting, for example, we discover that we are in the midst of that which is genuinely good. Our minds and hearts are turned from the unhealthy competitions and preoccupations of life as we attend to that which is fine and beautiful; moreover, in the midst of this, we oftentimes, particularly as persons of Christian faith, encounter in the work the presence of God and a reflection of the Divine. As Van Balthasar argues, all fine and beautiful things are in fact *epiphaneia*,[2] that which is glorious and a manifestation of the glory of God.

So, this newborn, newly created product of the human imagination leads away from the banal and repetitive in our ordinary experience. It typically leads away from a preoccupation with the spirit of competition, consumerism, violence, and degradation—and while I am not able at this point to digress concerning the question of the place of the ugly and evil in the world of art, I would note that the evil and ugly in human experience are also subject matter appropriate for artistic exploration. But that which is newborn and beautiful not only deflects from a preoccupation with the evil that surrounds us, but it also lays claim to goodness and truth. Beauty, newly created, bears witness to the goodness of God, and the possibility that the human heart may turn from the tyranny of a spirit of inhumanity and a spirit of bondage to evil and fear, toward a spirit of hope in a life with the resurrected Christ—hope for a life in which the beauty of God, and the beauty of the earth, is mirrored in the beauty of the church and its way of being in the world. The beautiful in nature and the beautiful that is the product of the human imagination are testaments to the glory of God and to God's love for all created beings and things. These things give witness to the possibilities that are ours, and nurture hope concerning the possibility for goodness, truth, and beauty in the midst of a broken and hostile world. These things, beauty and hope, lead the heart to desire, a desire that is fulfilled in the beauty of Christ and the hope of the church. Herein lies the transformation of the present.

In speaking of hope, Jürgen Moltmann argues that for the "Israelite and the Christian spirit . . . truth is found in the advent of that new thing which God has promised."[3] In both the Old and New Testaments,

---

2. Balthasar, *Glory of the Lord*, 1:11.
3. Moltmann, *Hope and Planning*, 182.

"the catchword of hope," he says, "is always the 'new.'" He elaborates on the themes of the new and Christian hope in this manner:

> As we look to participate in the kingdom of God, and participate in the shalom God chooses for us, we hear the exhortation of Christ, that we "Seek first the kingdom of God, and all these things shall be added unto you." Christian hope is rooted in the salvation and redemption that is ours as a consequence of the death and resurrection of Christ. Christian hope rests on this "Christ-event."[4]

The promise of the risen Christ is that he will come again and that there will be for us a new heaven and a new earth, in which we shall dwell with him for eternity. But, as we have noted, Christian hope not only anticipates this future, but it also strives for that which is now possible in the kingdom which God. As Moltmann puts it, "The prospect of this future coming from God already opens up here and now an open space of change and freedom which must be shaped with responsibility and confidence."[5] So, the work of artists and artisans contributes to this kingdom work of creating the beautiful as acts of freedom and responsibility, giving gifts to the church and the world of that which point beyond themselves and direct our minds and hearts toward God.

Walter Brueggemann makes the point that hope in the First Testament "is principally a this-worldly act." Israel remembers the gifts it has received from God in the past, gifts of progeny and land, gifts of miracles that sustained life and health. Consequently, they can therefore "hope for a new community of *shalom*, a new creation of well-being, and eventually a new personal destiny as a gift of God."[6] Moreover, this community of *shalom* in the parish or church community is intended to be a place of protection, what Brueggemann calls "a safe place for alternative hope that is crucial for the maintenance of a vibrant faith," in the face of a world defaced by "infidelity and despair."[7]

Now, I have spoken of participation in the beautiful as a mode of retreat, as a way in which it is possible to distance oneself from the facts of the givenness of our lives in order to center one's attention and will on the beautiful. And, we have referenced Brueggemann's idea of *shalom* as "a safe

---

4. Moltmann, *Hope and Planning*, 183.
5. Moltmann, *Hope and Planning*, 183.
6. Brueggemann, "Hope of Heaven," 99.
7. Brueggemann, "Hope of Heaven," 104.

place." However, as much as this notion of refuge and a safe place may seem to be self-centered and exclusionary of the exterior world, the separation that is spoken of here is not born of a centripetal impulse. For this is not a matter of retreating within oneself. It is, in fact, a matter of being outward looking, of creating new space, an enlarged space that is dominated by the beautiful and, therefore, filled with the love of God. Here, in this new space, we anticipate the new creation, the time when the prophet Habakkuk tells us that "the earth will be filled with the knowledge of the glory of the Lord, as the waters cover the sea" (Hab 2:14). As N. T. Wright suggests, "The world is beautiful not just because it hauntingly reminds us of its creator, but also because it is pointing forward: it is designed to be filled, flooded, drenched with God."[8] For the redeemed of God, this is what it is to participate in the beautiful: it is to be filled, flooded, and drenched with God, his beauty and goodness. Here, one experiences hope, for the form of the beautiful calls the eye and the heart of the Christian toward a vision of hope—hope for what can yet and will be. This is what it is to experience the manifestation of God in art and the beautiful, this is what epiphany suggests—the knowledge and hope of God through the encounter with this tide of love that fills and floods our being.

These experiences of the beautiful, when and as they are infused by love and visited by the Divine, both point to a time when all will be new and to a present when, in Christ, we experience *shalom*—a peace in which joy and fecundity are rooted in and nurtured by love and the very presence of the spirit of Christ. These moments are a harbinger of the time when God himself will "dwell among his people, filling the city with his life and love, pouring out grace and healing in the river of life that flows from the city out to the nations."[9] But it is important to note that such experience of glory and wonder is not merely a signpost of a future bliss that the redeemed of God anticipate in an afterlife. This is, in fact, part of what it is to experience the kingdom of God now, in the present. It is part of the experience of our salvation, that is, "our being raised to life in God's new heaven and new earth."[10] This is part of our healing and rescue, in which we receive the grace to glimpse the glory of God. This is the contribution of the beautiful to *shalom* and to the hope, as Christians, we have in Christ.

---

8. Wright, *Surprised by Hope*, 102.
9. Wright, *Surprised by Hope*, 105.
10. Wright, *Surprised by Hope*, 198.

SHALOM AND THE GIVING OF GIFTS

The community of *shalom*, marked by hope and the celebration of beauty, is also a community known for generosity and the giving of gifts, for, in these things, it mirrors the goodness and person of Christ. The giving of gifts takes many forms, including kindness shown to strangers, care of the lonely and bereaved, and feeding the hungry; these things we do in response to Jesus's command that we love one another and that we care for our neighbor and those we find alien to ourselves and our kin. In the context of this discussion of the arts and the place of the beautiful in the Christian life, I want to underscore the fact that the making of the beautiful is also a gift, whether we speak of music or any beautiful or fine object. The gift may be refined, it may be angular and spare, simple or complex; it may be the result of extensive and painstaking effort, or it may be ready at hand or easily constructed—the product of a few moments of labor but made possible by years of practice, like a piece of magnificent calligraphy by the hand of a practiced artist. It is a gift by virtue of its existence as the newborn and beautiful, whether it is physically gifted to another, displayed in a shop or gallery, or performed in a theater or concert hall.

Whatever the nature of the gift, the giving of gifts is a complicated matter, both with respect to the giver and to the receiver. Jacques Derrida, Marcel Mauss, Mary Douglas, and David Graeber, among others, testify to the complexity of the gift and the giving and receiving gifts in both ancient and contemporary societies. Douglas, in her foreword to Mauss's seminal work on the subject, *The Gift: The Form and Reason for Exchange in Archaic Societies*, argues that there is no such thing as a pure gift. "Right across the globe and as far back as we can go in the history of human civilization," she says, "the major transfer of goods has been cycles of obligatory returns of gifts."[11] Douglas goes on to report that after researching the system of gift-giving among a range of ancient societies, including various ancient legal systems—Roman, Germanic, and those of other Indo-European societies—all demonstrate that there are "no free gifts." "Gift cycles," she says, "engage persons in permanent commitments."[12] The idea of obligation and obligatory patterns and commitment is key to her assessment. Mauss, however, puts the anthropology of gift giving and receiving in a more favorable light. He summarizes the matter this way: "Societies have progressed in

---

11. Mary Douglas, in Mauss, *Gift*, viii.
12. Mary Douglas, in Mauss, *Gift*, ix.

so far as they themselves, their subgroups, and lastly, individuals in them, have succeeded in stabilizing relationships, giving, receiving, and finally, giving in return."[13] Where Douglas seems to emphasize the forcing of "permanent commitments," Mauss speaks of the principle significant outcome of gift giving as "stabilizing relationships."

Like Douglas, Derrida reacts to the potential forcing of a relational bond in consequence of the gift-giving cycle. He takes the position that the gift is possible, but only insofar as the donee "not give back, amortize, reimburse, acquit himself, enter into a contract." Indeed, he says, it is necessary that "he not *recognize* the gift as gift."[14] By way of contrast, Jacques Godbout and Alain Caillé, in a more recent piece of scholarship, take a somewhat different perspective on the gift and gift giving. They recognize the common rejection in the modern world of the idea of gift that assumes altruism or generosity on the part of the giver, suggesting that, for modern readers, the common response to the idea of gift is either to assume its "non-existence" or its "insubstantiality."[15] But, after rehearsing Mauss's findings of ancient societies and the "universality of the gift" in these societies, Godbout and Caillé argue that, in fact, contemporary research suggests that "the gift is just as typical of modern and contemporary societies as it is typical of archaic ones."[16] The gift, they observe, is "a matter not of dominating others or being dominated . . . but of belonging to a larger whole, of re-establishing a relationship, of becoming a member." They decry the inclination of Derrida and others to free themselves from ties with other people. "The modern individual, pseudo-emancipated from the duty of reciprocity, staggering under the accumulated weight of what she or he receives without making any return, becomes a great invalid, whose hypersensitivity makes it impossible to tolerate human relationships."[17] Godbout and Caillé's positive disposition to the concept of the gift and giving is consonant with the pattern of stable, mutually respectful, and caring relationships and communities that are characterized by the *shalom* of the Spirit of God.

But the concept of gift is elevated to a different plane altogether in Christian theology, in which the dimension of self-giving is critical to the concept of gift, self-giving being rooted in the sacrifice of Christ himself,

---

13. Mauss, *Gift*, 82.
14. Derrida, *Given Time*, 13.
15. Godbout and Caillé, *World of the Gift*, 4.
16. Godbout and Caillé, *World of the Gift*, 11.
17. Godbout and Caillé, *World of the Gift*, 220.

freely given for the love of the world. David Bentley Hart speaks of Christ's sacrifice as "a gift when it should not have needed to have been given again, by God, at a price that we imposed upon *him*." This love, he says, "defeats economy"; it is the "unanticipated grace of Easter."[18] How far this mode of gift exceeds the transactional pattern of Mauss's description of the patterns he observed! This is no longer a gift tied to obligation or the intent to stabilize a social structure through economic exchange; it is an act of grace, of unmerited favor. Hart expands on the nature of Christ's gift of himself. In a reference to Anselm on the topic of Christ's gift of himself, he makes the point that "the gift God gives in creation continues to be given again, ever more fully, in defiance of all rejection, economy, violence, and indifference." In this gift of himself, "there is no division between justice and mercy . . . because both belong already to the giving of this gift—which precedes, exceeds, and annuls all debt."[19] In a magnificent statement regarding the nature and healing purposes of Christ's sacrifice, Hart makes the point that "Christ, who suffers outside the gate, makes of his death an act of inclusion that begins the world anew; his resurrection erases the boundary between city and waste, life and death, pure and impure, exclusion and inclusion, by simply passing these distinctions by in his infinite motion toward the Father."[20]

This language and concept of gift encompasses Godbout and Caillé's understanding of gift as a means of reestablishing relationship and contributing to mutuality in community; but, in speaking of gift in terms of God's gift of himself to humanity, the model for understanding gift is radically enlarged. It is now utterly selfless; it stands in the face of rejection and indifference. It is a model of the giver whose nature is to give fully of himself out of love for the other. It is a model of humility and of obedience. Christ's gift of himself, an act that invites and invokes newness, transforms entirely our understanding of what the gift and gift-giving process can be, even in the context of human intercourse. The understanding of gift as a means of establishing and reestablishing relationships and maintaining a stable social structure is ultimately inadequate as a means of transcending human frailty, deceit, and brokenness. It is only the gift of Christ that makes possible human salvation and transformation; and it is the radical selfless

---

18. Hart, *Beauty of the Infinite*, 371.
19. Hart, *Beauty of the Infinite*, 372.
20. Hart, *Beauty of the Infinite*, 385.

giving that Christ models that is the basis of the giving and loving to which the church is called.

We recognize that the gifts we offer each other and God, as Christians, is of an entirely different order than God's gift of himself; yet God's gift of himself provides a model for how we might understand gift in the context of a community of *shalom*. We are to give with the intent of blessing and nurturing the other, recognizing that such giving may not be reciprocated nor appreciated. We are to give out of a posture of humility rather than out of a prideful heart. We give our music, art, and artistry out of a posture of love for the other, irrespective of the other's economic or social position, race or faith, and irrespective of the other's apparent wholeness or obvious brokenness. And we recognize that, in the gift of the beautiful, we point others to the superabundant goodness and grace of God who makes possible the creation of beauty and the appreciation of the beautiful in a broken world.

On a personal note, throughout the years during which I was active as a conductor, I gave gifts of my musical imagination and craft in my rehearsals and performances. While preparing for a concert tour in Italy, I sought for a performance edition of various of the magnificent psalm settings of Sweelinck. Discovering that these particular psalm settings were unavailable in a performing edition, I made trips to the British Museum and the Bodleian Library in Oxford to prepare an edition of three settings, which I then performed with my chamber ensemble in Rome, Assisi, and Venice. This is not an uncommon narrative. It is oftentimes part of the work and vocation of artistic directors of choral ensembles to transcribe and/or edit music for performance purposes. The point is that this particular activity of preparing a performing edition, and the subsequent performance of this material, was part of a cycle of giving and receiving gifts: Sweelinck's gift to the ages, my gift to my singers of his work, their gift to me of exquisite and imaginative music-making, and the presentation of this artistic product to an audience—all of this constituted a series of gifts and gift giving. This giving of gifts begins with the giving of the musical self as a labor of love and sacrifice, intended as a gift and a blessing to those who witness and receive the gift.

Parenthetically, there is an additional benefit and evidence of the Spirit of God to be found in this domain of the giving and receiving of gifts; I think here specifically of gifts of an artistic nature. The collective striving for excellence in an artistic project, whether that is related to liturgical worship or some other endeavor, often leads to the cultivation of friendships. Where these friendships are based on spiritual as well as artistic goals and interests, one often discovers the development of spiritual friendship. Aelred of Rievaulx, a medieval Cistercian abbot, in a volume entitled *Spiritual Friendship*, speaks of the manner in which such friendships enable us to transcend our subjectivity, our inward-lookingness, and recognize our need for interrelatedness. This is part of what a community marked by *shalom* is like. Such friendships, rooted in love and mutuality, are part of a larger tapestry of the spiritual community that seeks to honor God in its worship and praise and its way of being.

NOTES FOR THE CHURCH

With respect to the life of the church and the individual's spiritual life in Christ, I want to address the matter of the gift and the giving of gifts with particular attention to the integrity of our labor where the gift is a product of our craft. The noteworthiness of the integrity of labor rests on the fact that, at its heart, integrity of labor is a matter of Christian faithfulness. The faithful execution of one's craft pertains to the desire to give one's best to God. This attitude of doing what is best and right within artistic practice, whatever the discipline, is, in fact, a response to the ethical demands of artistic practice, practice that assumes that there is always a range of artistic and technical options open to the craftsperson, not all of which lead to the production of a fine and beautiful product, and not all of which are among the choices of one who intends to give his or her best in the creation of the product or work. This, of course, marks the confluence of ethics and aesthetics. In some, if not many, instances, the recipients of such gifts who are not expert in the discipline may be unaware of an artistically shoddy decision and its impact on the outcome. But in the light of a gift given as a gift of oneself and one's talent, the process of the making is of genuine importance. The process itself must be artistically faithful in order to be consonant with the overarching feature of *shalom*, where the peace of God impacts peoples' relationships with each other, with God, and with themselves. The integrity of one's action as an artist or craftsperson is critical to this peace, for it is rooted in right action and is therefore foundational to the Christian intention to seek and find Christ in all things.

As our work and way of accomplishing this work is dedicated to Christ, it becomes not only a sacrifice of labor and love but a service consecrated to *him*. As such, the way of doing our work and living out our vocation is of critical importance. If one's work is slothful, it hardly constitutes an appropriate offering of one's labor and talents. Where in the process of doing our work, we are readily satisfied with the mediocre, our lack of fervor and integrity indicates a lack of fidelity. If we are to commune with God through our action, our work must be animated by the desire to offer to God the best of our talents, energy, spirit, and intellect. This is our gift of love to *him*, and, simultaneously, it is a gift of hope and peace to the world in which we live. In this way, we also put on Christ; in this way, we are agents of God's grace.

Further to this point, I recall Thomas Merton's reference to the poetry of Dylan Thomas. His integrity as a poet, says Merton, "makes me very ashamed of the verse I have been writing." The point is not that the shame to which Merton alludes is due to possessing a lesser talent than Thomas. He speaks of the effort of Thomas's struggle with the text until the text is polished and honed, until it speaks with the voice the poet intends. This, of course, is the process essential to the poet as artist. Merton's self-confessed shame, whether or not overstated, serves his purpose of underscoring the need of a rigorous standard of personal and artistic excellence. And so he addresses himself as well as his readers when he says "We who say we love God: why are we not so anxious to be perfect in our art as we pretend to want to be in our service of God?" Merton continues to say, "If we do not try to be perfect in what we write, perhaps it is because we are not writing for God after all."[21]

In theological terms, what we have been speaking of is the sanctification of our activities, including our craft. When we as believers engage in artistic activity in the context of praise and worship, we offer our talents as a gift to God. What we offer is, of course, not only the art or craft of our hands and voices; first and foremost, what we offer is an authentic emotional and intellectual response to God. It is an expressive, creative, and spiritual act that signifies our love of God, that expresses gratefulness, that articulates the passions that characterize our human condition and our response to God. This activity we consecrate to God, as we consecrate all our daily activities to *him*. This involves actively seeking and finding Christ in all we do, in dedicating our action to him as service and ourselves as sacrifice. It draws on the idea of honest labor and a labor that is characterized by all the technical, imaginative, and artistic refinement of which we are capable. It establishes as a necessary condition of

---

21. Merton, *Thomas Merton Reader*, 249.

sanctified labor the integrity of the workman, whether that is the work of the scholar, laborer, or artist. This we do to honor and glorify God; we offer our work as a gift of love to the One who first loved us.

8

Epilogue

During the preceding chapters, we have explored the question of the value of the arts in the Christian life and the life of the church and have presented several of the more compelling theories of art that are part of the Western philosophical tradition, which speak to the question of where such value is to be found and how it is to be understood. Whatever philosophical view one adopts—formalist, expressionist, symbolist, or other—it is generally agreed that human experience is, in some way, enriched by interaction with imaginative worlds that are the product of the artist. Engagement in these works provides an escape from the routine of common experience and entry into new worlds of music, theater, visual art, poetry, and literature, which elevates our experience by the sheer splendor of the work and its way of being. As previously noted, Kierkegaard argues that all men are created in such a manner that they have the possibility to become more fully human than they now are. For the Christian, this process of becoming affects the full range of our human capacities: intellectual, imaginative, emotional, and spiritual. We recognize that much of our lives are spent in what the American Episcopalian Frederick Buechner refers to as "an unenchanted forest," where every tree is a task to be completed and in which the replicative functioning and requirements of daily existence characterize much of our life. Participation in the arts provides opportunity for release from the oppression of the immediate. Rather like the children in C. S. Lewis's *Narnia* stories who enter a new and wonderful world through the back of the wardrobe, the art world offers entrance into new worlds, more imaginatively rich, compelling, textured, and dynamic than our commonplace reality.

The question is what this has to do with what has been spoken of as the process of becoming, in Christ; what has this to do with the Christian life? I suggest that we need to see our salvation, first, as union with God made possible by forgiveness of sin, through the salvific work of Christ; and, second, as a call to wholeness that involves a transformational process by which we become more fully human, as God intended us to be. We need to reclaim the psalmist's view of the earth as a vibrant and glorious home, created by the Holy One for his pleasure and ours; we need to reclaim our human capacity for imaginative experience and apply these capacities to an abundant life of praise and worship, where all we do is given over to Christ, and our lives become a sacrifice pleasing to our Lord and Creator. Surely, the enrichment of human experience offered by participation in these beautiful and imaginative worlds is part of living a whole life, a life of abundance that God has ordained for us. This is, in my view, part of God's grace and the bounty of *shalom*, in which we experience peace and wholeness as a blessing and gift of God.

Indeed, living a life that is imaginatively engaged and rich I take to be characteristic of a life of praise to him who provided this world of beauty, integrity, multiplicity, and variety for his creatures. Our salvation involves both our redemption and our transformation. The latter enables us to embrace the good, the true, and the beautiful. It frees us to revel in the magnificence of the creation and in the joy there is found in creating, for this is characteristic of the Creator himself. This capacity has been given to us for our pleasure and his.

We are called to life: and part of that is a call to the full expression of our humanity, which includes exploring and exercising our artistic and aesthetic capacities. This is part of a whole life, a new life in the kingdom of God. To live out of the hand of the Father, to live in a manner that exercises our imaginative and creative gifts, to be appreciative of the art-making and symbol-making of others is to live a life of praise.

For the believer, art-making is a mode of worship and praise. Art-making is world-making that involves the construction of imaginative worlds of words, pictures, actions, images, and movement that are often of great seriousness and import. This is a means by which we offer praise and sacrifice of our talents to the Almighty. It is not a casual enterprise, as

EPILOGUE

Merton has noted. It requires giving the best of our imaginative, artistic, and technical abilities to the glory of God.

All of life, all of the life of one committed thoroughly to Christ, is worship. Living a life that is appreciative of and engaged in the beautiful is an appropriate part of this redeemed and transformed life, lived to the glory of God. A life in the exercising of our imaginative faculties for the purpose of designing a bridge, a stained glass window, or a kite becomes an expression of worship when dedicated to the Father and when offered as sacrifice of our talents, our time, our being to the Lord.

To witness to the world of the salvation that is ours in Christ lies at the very heart of the Christian life. This witness rests on the evidence of new life, the transformed life of individuals and of the corporate life of the church. So, out of the abundance of the good gifts the Father has given, we compose songs, hymns, and chants; we paint, write plays, dance, and sing; and we revel in the glorious artistic work of others. For as we seek and find Christ in all of this, God is glorified, and herein lies the very purpose of our being.

Bibliography

Aquinas, Thomas. *Summa Theologiae*. Edited by John Mortensen and Enrique Alarcon. Translated by Fr. Laurence Shapcote. Lander, WY: Aquinas Institute for the Study of Sacred Doctrine, 2012.

Aristotle. *Rhetoric*. Translated by John Henry Freese. Cambridge, MA: Harvard University Press, 1926.

Augustine. *Confessions*. Translated by Henry Chadwick. Oxford, UK: Oxford University Press, 1998.

Balthasar, Hans Urs von. *Seeing the Form*. Vol. 1 of *The Glory of the Lord: A Theological Aesthetics*. Edited by Joseph Fessio and John Riches. Translated by Erasmo Leiva-Merikakis. San Francisco: Ignatius, 1982.

———. *Studies in Theological Style*. Vol. 2 of *The Glory of the Lord: A Theological Aesthetics*. Edited by John Riches. Translated by Andrew Louth et al. San Francisco: Ignatius, 1984.

Barney, Rachel. "Notes on Plato on the *Kalon* and the Good." *Classical Philology* 105 (2010) 363–77.

Beardsley, Munroe. *The Aesthetic Point of View*. Ithaca, NY: Cornell University Press, 1982.

———. *Aesthetics: Problems in the Philosophy of Criticism*. Indianapolis: Hackett, 1981.

Bell, Clive. *Art*. London: Chatto and Windus, 1914.

Benedict XVI, Pope. "Meeting of the Holy Father Benedict XVI with the Clergy of the Diocese of Bolzano-Bressanone." Vatican, Aug. 6, 2008. https://www.vatican.va/content/benedict-xvi/en/speeches/2008/august/documents/hf_ben-xvi_spe_20080806_clero-bressanone.html.

Black, Max. *Models and Metaphors*. Ithaca, NY: Cornell University Press, 1962.

Brooks, Cleanth. *The Well Wrought Urn: Studies in the Structure of Poetry*. London: Dobson, 1968.

Brueggemann, Walter. "The Hope of Heaven . . . on Earth." *Biblical Theological Bulletin* 29 (1999) 99–111.

Buelow, George J. "Affects, Theory of the." *Grove Music Online*, 2001. https://doi.org/10.1093/gmo/9781561592630.article.00253.

Chomksy, Noam. *Language and Mind*. Cambridge: Cambridge University Press, 2006.

Coates, A. M. "Beauty Lived towards Shalom: The Christian Life as Aesthetic-Ethical Existence." *Acta Theologica* 29 (2020) 93–113.

Coleridge, Samuel Taylor. *Biographia Literaria, Chapters I–IV, XIV–XXII*. With *Prefaces and Essays on Poetry, 1800–1815*, by William Wordsworth. Edited by George Sampson. Cambridge: Cambridge University Press, 1920.

BIBLIOGRAPHY

Collinson, Diane. "Aesthetic Experience." In *Philosophical Aesthetics: An Introduction*, edited by Oswald Hanfling, 111–78. Oxford, UK: Blackwell, 1992.

Cooke, Deryck. *The Language of Music*. London: Oxford University Press, 1959.

Copland, Aaron. *Music and Imagination*. Cambridge, MA: Harvard University Press, 1952.

Danto, Arthur. *The Transfiguration of the Commonplace*. Cambridge: Cambridge University Press, 1981.

Davison, Julian. *Balinese Architecture*. Hong Kong: Periplus, 2003.

Derrida, Jacques. *Given Time: 1. Counterfeit Money*. Translated by Peggy Kamuf. Chicago: University of Chicago Press, 1992.

Ducasse, Curt John. "The Aesthetic Attitude." In *The Problems of Aesthetics*, edited by Eliseo Vivas and Murray Krieger, 358–68. New York: Holt, Rinehart and Winston, 1953.

Eco, Umberto. *The Aesthetics of Thomas Aquinas*. Translated by Hugh Bredin. York, UK: Radius, 1988.

Eliot, T. S. *The Use of Poetry and the Use of Criticism*. London: Faber and Faber, 1933.

Farrell, Edward J. *Beams of Prayer: Spiritual Reflections with Edward J. Farrell*. Compiled and edited by Lynn L. Salata. New York: Alba House, 1999.

Fry, Roger. *Vision and Design*. London: Chatto and Windus, 1920.

Frye, Northrop. *Anatomy of Criticism: Four Essays*. Princeton, NJ: Princeton University Press, 1957.

———. *The Educated Imagination*. Toronto: Canadian Broadcasting Corporation, 1963.

———. *The Educated Imagination and Other Selected Writings in Critical Theory 1933–1963*. Toronto: University of Toronto Press, 2016.

———. *T. S. Eliot: An Introduction*. Chicago: Chicago University Press, 1963.

Garcia-Rivera, Alejandro. *The Community of the Beautiful: A Theological Aesthetics*. Collegeville, MN: Liturgical Press, 1999.

Godbout, Jacques, and Alain Caillé. *The World of the Gift*. Translated by Donald Winkler. Montreal: McGill-Queen's University Press, 2000.

Goodman, Nelson. *Languages of Art*. Indianapolis: Hackett, 1976.

———. *Problems and Projects*. New York: Bobbs-Merrill, 1972.

Gracyk, Theodore. "Hume's Aesthetics." Stanford Encyclopedia of Philosophy, Dec. 17, 2003; revised Apr. 21, 2020. https://plato.stanford.edu/entries/hume-aesthetics/.

Hall, James. *Dictionary of Subjects and Symbols in Art*. 2nd ed. Boulder, CO: Westview, 2008.

Hanfling, Oswald, ed. *Philosophical Aesthetics: An Introduction*. Oxford, UK: Blackwell, 1992.

Hannay, Alastair. *Kierkegaard: Arguments of the Philosophers*. London: Routledge & Kegan Paul, 1982.

Hanslick, Eduard. *On the Musically Beautiful*. Translated and edited by Geoffrey Payzant. Indianapolis: Hackett, 1986.

Hardy, I. Gusti Ngurah Wiras, and Aplimon Jerobisonif. "Makna Simbolis *Kori Agung* Dalam Kehidupan Ritual Masyarakat Hindu di Bali." *Gewang* 2 (Apr. 2020) 16–22.

Harnoncourt, Nikolaus. *The Musical Dialogue: Thoughts on Monteverdi, Bach and Mozart*. Translated by Mary O'Neill. Portland, OR: Amadeus, 1984.

Harrison, Carol. *Beauty and Revelation in the Thought of Saint Augustine*. Oxford, UK: Clarendon, 1992.

BIBLIOGRAPHY

Hart, David Bentley. *The Beauty of the Infinite: The Aesthetics of Christian Truth.* Grand Rapids: Eerdmanns, 2003.

Hausman, Carl R. *Metaphor and Art: Interactionism and Reference in the Verbal and Nonverbal Arts.* Cambridge: Cambridge University Press, 1989.

Hawkes, Terence. *Structuralism and Semiotics.* Oakland, CA: University of California Press, 1977.

Hegel, Georg Wilhelm Friedrich. "Vorlesungen über die Asthetik." In *Musical Aesthetics: A Historical Reader,* edited by Edward Lippman, 2:85–161. New York: Pendragon, 1988.

Henle, Paul, ed. "Metaphor." In *Language, Thought and Culture,* edited by Paul Henle, 173–95. Ann Arbor: University of Michigan Press, 1958.

Hindemith, Paul. *A Composer's World: Horizons and Limitations.* Charles Eliot Norton Lectures, 1949–1950. Cambridge, MA: Harvard University Press, 1952.

Hirst, Paul. *Knowledge and the Curriculum: A Collection of Philosophical Papers.* London: Routledge and Kegan Paul, 1974.

Hospers, John. *An Introduction to Philosophical Analysis.* Englewood Cliffs, NJ: Prentice-Hall, 1967.

Hume, David. *The Philosophical Works of David Hume.* Edited by T. H. Green and T. H. Grose. London: Longmans, Green, 1875.

Hungerland, Isabel Creed. "Once Again, Aesthetic and Non-Aesthetic." In *Aesthetics,* edited by Harold Osborne, 106–20. Oxford, UK: Oxford University Press, 1972.

Ingarden, Roman. "Artistic and Aesthetic Values." In *Aesthetics,* edited by Harold Osborne, 39–54. Oxford, UK: Oxford University Press, 1972.

John of the Cross. *The Collected Works of Saint John of the Cross.* Translated by Kieran Kavanaugh and Otilio Rodriguez. Washington, DC: Institute of Carmelite Studies, 1991.

Kant, Immanuel. *Critique of Judgment.* Translated by James Creed Meredith. Oxford, UK: Oxford University Press, 1952.

Kerman, Joseph. *Contemplating Music: Challenges to Musicology.* Cambridge, MA: Harvard University Press, 1985.

Kittay, Eva Feder. *Metaphor: Its Cognitive Force and Linguistic Structure.* Oxford, UK: Oxford University Press, 1987.

Lang, Paul Henry. *Music in Western Civilization.* New York: Norton, 1941.

Langer, Suzanne K. *Feeling and Form: A Theory of Art.* New York: Scribner's, 1953.

Lewis, C. S. *An Experiment in Criticism.* Cambridge: Cambridge University Press, 1961.

Lippman, Edward. *A History of Western Musical Aesthetics.* Lincoln: University of Nebraska Press, 1992.

Mahler, Gustav. *Das Lied von der Erde: Eine Symphonie fur eine Tenor-und eine Alt- (oder Bariton-) Stimme und Orchester.* Translated by Hans Bethge. Vienna: Universal, 1990.

Maritain, Jacques. *Art and Scholasticism.* Translated by J. F. Scanlan. London: Sheed and Ward, 1947.

Martner, Knud, ed. *Selected Letters of Gustav Mahler.* Translated by Eithne Wilkins et al. London: Faber and Faber, 1979.

Mauss, Marcel. *The Gift: The Form and Reason for Exchange in Archaic Societies.* Translated by W. D. Halls. New York: Norton, 1990.

McCormick, Peter J. *Modernity, Aesthetics, and the Bounds of Art.* Ithaca, NY: Cornell University Press, 1990.

Bibliography

Merton, Thomas. *A Thomas Merton Reader.* Compiled by Thomas P. McDonnell. New York: Image, 1974.

Meyer, Leonard. *Emotion and Meaning in Music.* Chicago: University of Chicago Press, 1956.

Moltmann, Jürgen. *Hope and Planning.* London: SCM, 1971.

Moore, George Edward. *Principia Ethica.* Cambridge: Cambridge University Press, 1903.

Mothersill, Mary. *Beauty Restored.* Oxford, UK: Clarendon, 1984.

Mulyaningrum, S. E. "Bali: The Island of a Thousand Puras." Dr. Mulyaningrum, Aug. 24, 2014. https://mulyaningrum.wordpress.com/2014/08/24/bali-the-island-of-a-thousand-puras/.

Nichols, Aidan. *A Key to Balthasar: Hans Urs von Balthasar on Beauty, Goodness, and Truth.* Grand Rapids: Baker Academic, 2011.

———. *Redeeming Beauty: Soundings in Sacral Aesthetics.* Aldershot, UK: Ashgate, 2007.

Norris, Christopher. *Deconstruction: Theory and Practice.* London: Routledge, 1991.

Paivio, Allan. "Psychological Processes in the Comprehension of Metaphor." In *Metaphor and Thought*, edited by Andrew Ortony, 150–71. Cambridge: Cambridge University Press, 1979.

Palmer, Richard, E. *Hermeneutics: Interpretation Theory in Schleiermacher, Dilthey, Heidegger, and Gadamer.* Evanston, IL: Northwestern University Press, 1969.

Panofsky, Erwin. *Meaning in the Visual Arts.* Garden City, NY: Doubleday, 1955.

Phelan, G. B. *G. B. Phelan: Selected Papers.* Toronto: Pontifical Institute of Mediaeval Studies, 1967.

Plato. *Republic.* Edited by G. R. Ferrari. Translated by Tom Griffith. Cambridge: Cambridge University Press, 2000.

———. *Symposium.* Translated by B. Jowett. Princeton, NJ: Van Nostrand, 1942.

Plotinus. *The Enneads.* Translated by Stephen MacKenna. London: Penguin, 1991.

Plutarch. *Plutarch's Lives.* Edited by A. H. Clough. Translated by John Dryden. New York: Nottingham Society, n.d.

Porter, Jean. *The Recovery of Virtue.* Louisville, KY: Westminster John Knox, 1990.

Proust, Marcel. *Remembrance of Things Past.* Vol.1. Translated by C. K. Scott Moncrieff. Harmondsworth, UK: Penguin, 2017.

Putra, Diasana. "The Balinese Palaces in Gianyar: Representing Authority Power and Creating Territorial Identity." *International Journal of Innovation, Creativity and Change* 14 (2020) 132–50.

Reid, Louis Arnaud. *Ways of Knowledge and Experience.* London: Allen & Unwin, 1961.

Richards, I. A. *Philosophy of Rhetoric.* London: Oxford University Press, 1936.

Rieser, Max. "The Semantic Theory of Art in America." *Journal of Aesthetics and Art Criticism* 15 (1956) 12–26.

Rorty, Richard. "Intuition." In *The Encyclopedia of Philosophy*, edited by Paul Edwards, 4: 204–12. New York: Macmillan, 1967.

Rubin, Michael. "The Meaning of 'Beauty' and its Transcendental Status in the Metaphysics of Thomas Aquinas." PhD diss., Catholic University of America, 2019.

Russell, Lewis. *Thinking about Music: An Introduction to the Philosophy of Music.* Amherst: University of Massachusetts Press, 1984.

Santayana, George. *The Life of Reason: Reason in Art.* London: Constable, 1905.

Sartwell, Crispin. "Beauty." Stanford Encyclopedia of Philosophy, Sept. 4, 2012; revised Oct. 5, 2016. https://plato.stanford.edu/archives/win2017/entries/beauty/.

BIBLIOGRAPHY

Schindler, Anton Felix. *Beethoven as I Knew Him*. Edited by Donald W. MacArdle. Translated by Constance Jolly. London: Faber and Faber, 1966.
Schopenhauer, Arthur. "Die Welt als Wille und Vorstellung." In *Musical Aesthetics: A Historical Reader*, edited by Edward Lippman, 2:163–92. New York: Pendragon, 1988.
Screech, M. A. *Ecstasy & The Praise of Folly*. London: Penguin, 1980.
Scruton, Roger. *The Aesthetics of Architecture*. Princeton, NJ: Princeton University Press, 1980.
Sevier, Christopher Scott. *Aquinas on Beauty*. Lanham, MD: Lexington, 2015.
Soskice, Janet. *Metaphor and Religious Language*. Oxford, UK: Clarendon, 1985.
Steiner, Peter. *Russian Formalism: A Metapoetics*. Ithaca, NY: Cornell University Press, 1984.
Teilhard de Chardin, Pierre. *The Divine Milieu*. New York: Harper & Row, 1960.
Tolstoy, Leo. *What Is Art?* Translated by Aylmer Maude. London: Walter Scott, 1899.
Tourangeau, Roger. "Metaphor and Cognitive Structure." In *Metaphor: Problems and Perspectives*, edited by David S. Miall, 14–35. Brighton, UK: Humanities, 1982.
Treitler, Leo. *Music and the Historical Imagination*. Cambridge, MA: Harvard University Press, 1989.
Verbrugge, Robert R., and Nancy S. McCarrell. "Metaphoric Comprehension: Studies in Reminding and Resembling." *Cognitive Psychology* 9 (1977) 494–533.
Viladesau, Richard. *Theological Aesthetics: God in Imagination, Beauty, and Art*. New York: Oxford University Press, 1999.
Wagner, Richard. *Opera and Drama*. Translated by William Ashton Ellis. Lincoln: University of Nebraska Press, 1995.
Wayan, Michael. "Church Palasari: Western End of Bali." Palasari Community, Dec. 29, 2002. https://infoinbali.blogspot.com.
Welsh, Paul. "Discursive and Presentational Symbols." *Mind* 64 (1955) 181–89.
Wimsatt, William K. *The Verbal Icon: Studies in the Meaning of Poetry*. Lexington: University of Kentucky Press, 1954.
Wolterstorff, Nicholas. *Educating for Shalom: Essays on Christian Higher Education*. Grand Rapids: Eerdmans, 2004.
Wordsworth, William. *Prefaces and Essays on Poetry, 1800–1815*. With *Biographia Literaria, Chapters I–IV, XIV–XXII*, by Samuel Taylor Coleridge. Edited by George Sampson. Cambridge: Cambridge University Press, 1920.
Wright, N. T. *Surprised by Hope: Rethinking Heaven, the Resurrection, and the Mission of the Church*. New York: HarperOne, 2008.
Zarlino, Gioseffe. "Instituzioni armoniche." In *Source Readings in Music History: The Renaissance*, edited by Oliver Strunk, 38–71. New York: Norton, 1965.